GIVE
YOURSELF
CREDIT:
The Art of Borrowing

THE DREYFUS FAMILY MONEY MANAGEMENT SERVICE

GIVE YOURSELF CREDIT:

The Art of Borrowing

by MARTIN MAYER
and the Editors of Dreyfus Publications

illustrated by Roy Doty

DREYFUS PUBLICATIONS LTD.,   NEW YORK

MARTIN MAYER is a writer known for definitive publications on a number of subjects. Among his books are *Wall Street: Men and Money, The Schools, New Breed on Wall Street, Madison Avenue, U.S.A., The Lawyers,* and *About Television.* After studying economics at Harvard he worked for a time at the *New York Journal of Commerce.* He has written for many magazines, including *Dun's Review* and *Fortune* in the field of business.

DREYFUS PUBLICATIONS LTD.

Jerome S. Hardy
PRESIDENT

Sally J. Reich
Martin Stone
VICE-PRESIDENTS

THE DREYFUS FAMILY MONEY MANAGEMENT SERVICE

Jay Gold, Editorial Director
Earle G. Kersh, Design Consultant

Heinz Eller, Publisher
John C. Tosarello, Marketing Manager
Rosalie Bruno, Business Manager

CONTENTS

A NOTE TO THE READER

This book has been designed to be as functional as it is informative. The typographic design for the text calls for exceptionally wide margins. These are meant to be used for notes, reminders to yourself, or arithmetical calculations. The editors hope you will use them for these purposes.

The stock for this book was selected in part because it can be written on equally well with pencil, ink pen, ball-point or felt-tipped pen.

As Mr. Mayer trenchantly points out in Chapter II, "Borrowing and Coming Out Ahead," "*Your* situation must be the key to your decision." Use the space in the margins to make notes on *your* particular situation as you go along.

As one step in this direction, colored rules have been used to emphasize salient portions of the text.

—THE EDITORS

Time was that credit was feared as
a veritable man-eater. Nowadays it is considered
a nice pussycat to have around—if properly
housebroken and otherwise looked after.

CHAPTER I

Credit, Credit Everywhere

If an American who died 60 years ago could be brought back to visit his great-great-grandchildren today, there'd be no end to the things that would surprise him.

The development of inventions that were just off the drawing boards in his time—automobiles and airplanes, radio and skyscrapers—would amaze him, and television he would see as a miracle. The settlement of the country, the way the population center has moved all the way out beyond the Mississippi, would startle him. And the fact that most people are so well off would bowl him over.

But as he settled in with his descendants, a young couple in their late twenties, with two children and a house in the suburbs, the man of the family working in one of those office jobs that have become so common, our old-timer might find himself puzzled and troubled by one aspect of modern life that would have terrified any sensible man in his generation—the fact that the family is in debt, and so are all the neighbors, and nobody seems worried about it.

Credit, once a man-eating tiger that seemed to threaten everyone, has become in our time a domestic pet, easy for almost everyone to keep and enjoy. The fact is that the country runs on credit. Increasingly, employers don't pay their workers in cash and

One of the reasons bankers prefer to lend money to businesses rather than to individuals
is that a business uses the loan for business purposes.
Personal loans are often used for monkey business.

people don't pay their bills in cash—purchases for everything but day-to-day needs are made either on a buy-now-pay-later basis or with a check. And the check, more often than not, will have somewhere in its ancestry a loan made by a bank.

You know how much trouble you would have buying a new car if you could not pay for it in installments. What you may not realize is that a breakdown in the credit system would very quickly mean that you couldn't find a new car to buy. The car dealer can keep cars in his showroom only because a bank or a finance company is willing to finance his inventory. The manufacturer who machines the cylinders for the engines relies on credit to buy the steel he

uses. The independent trucker who carries the steel from the mill to the manufacturer owns the truck he uses only because somebody was willing to lend him the purchase price.

Altogether, about 60% of the "money" circulating in the United States today is bank credit.

Of course, your situation in buying a family car is significantly different from that of the manufacturer who bores cylinders for engines. He's borrowing "working capital," and he'll pay back his borrowings as soon as he sells his cylinders to the automobile manufacturer. His is a *business* loan, which means that the purpose for which the loan is made relates to the way it will be repaid. Yours is a *personal* loan, which means that the loan will be repaid out of earnings that have nothing to do with your reasons for borrowing the money.

A banker's preference in customers

Even though consumer loans are more profitable than business loans for most banks, when money is tight a banker would rather lend to the manufacturer than to you. For a number of reasons: because he can be more certain that the manufacturer will pay him back; because the manufacturer is a steady customer who can be counted on to borrow at the same season every year; and because business-loan rates go up faster in tight-money periods than consumer-loan rates. The banker expresses this preference by charging you a much higher interest rate than he charges for most business loans.

There are many different kinds of credit (short or long term, secured or unsecured), to be used for different purposes (to pay the butcher or carry the inventory of a store or buy the raw

Money can be had at any number of different price tags. The cost depends on many things: among them, the purpose of the loan, your credit standing, the state of the credit markets at the time.

material used in a factory) and paid for at different interest rates (all the way from 5% to 36% a year). But from one point of view all credit is the same: Credit enables borrowers to buy or do something they wouldn't be able to buy or do if they had to pay cash.

All credit except loans within families or between friends (and even here you want to be careful about how you "put yourself in debt" to somebody) will involve repaying to the lender more than he originally loaned you. And all credit rests on the lender's belief that the borrower will in fact be able to repay the loan.

Long ago, money and credit had a mysterious, even sinful aura. Religious leaders denounced charging interest on loans: interest was "usury." England and America had special debtors laws, and even debtors prisons to punish those who had borrowed money and couldn't pay it back. (A lot of what the novelist Charles Dickens thought about the world, and particularly of business, was influenced by the fact that when he was a boy his father was locked up in a debtors prison.)

The lender's unrequited love

Not so long ago, mortgages on farms and homes were written in such a way that all of the loan fell due on one feared day, when the lender might or might not renew the loan. If he wouldn't write a new mortgage and the family couldn't pay off the remaining debt, the lender could collect the security pledged to the loan. In the language of the time, he could "foreclose" the property, take away the family farm, if for any reason (even unrequited love for the farmer's daughter) he chose to do so. Shakespeare's Shylock, who gave a name to the unscrupulous

In the Bad Old Days, before the creation of the self-amortizing loan, the day the mortgage became due was not regarded lightly by the mortgagee.

lender, could demand a pound of flesh. Under these circumstances, the Puritan ethic that forbade "going into debt" made a lot of sense, and parents were right to warn their children against buying anything before they "could afford it." In the modern world, that warning does not hold true.

There's no doubt that reckless borrowing can make life miserable for people who haven't thought about how they are going to repay their loans. Talking to a group of student teachers in Brooklyn not long ago, a judge begged them to get across to their pupils *somehow*, as one thing city dwellers in particular have to bear in mind, that anyone who buys on the installment plan not only has to make the first payment but will have to keep making the payments until the loan is all paid back.

It's not just the first payment

A lawyer in Florida tells heartbreaking stories about semi-retired people who were oversold by advertising for a franchise ice-cream business or dry-cleaning establishment or motel, and borrowed the money to buy the franchise: they did not realize that because they were buying with borrowed money they would have to work much longer hours than friends who had started similar businesses with their own savings. The money their friends could use to pay help (or the sales their friends could pass up by closing early) they would need to pay back the bank.

But the ordinary man who knows what he's doing,

and knows how he's going to earn the money to pay back his loan, can be just as prudent and successful a borrower as the industrialist who relies on the bank to supply him with working capital.

The important thing in borrowing is to know what you're doing.

A common mistake: borrowing money to pay for a franchise. The loan makes the franchise a lead weight instead of a comfort to one's semi-retirement years.

CHAPTER II

Borrowing—and Coming Out Ahead

Not long ago, a veteran living in a suburb of St. Louis gave an old-fashioned kind of party, at which he burned in the barbecue the 20-year $11,000 mortgage he had taken to buy a $14,000 house shortly after his return from the Korean War. One of his friends at the party was a real estate broker, who asked him whether he might want to sell the house, now that he owned it free and clear. Playing along with the joke, the veteran said he might be interested: what was he offered? And the real estate broker, who knew the current values in the neighborhood, said $39,000.

Adding up all the interest payments he had made to the bank over the past 20 years (at 5½ %, the rate in the early 1950s), the veteran found that the house had cost him in total, including the cost of his mortgage, less than $22,000. In fact, adding up all the heating bills and plumbing bills and painting bills and water taxes and school taxes and city taxes, even including the finishing of the basement room and the new room for Julie, the third child, the veteran figured out, late that night, that if he sold his house

A mortgage loan can easily be a painless, because unnoticed, way of making money over a long haul because of the appreciation in suburban housing values.

he and his wife could honestly say they and their children had lived in it for 20 years almost for free.

In fact, he would make it somewhat better than free, because the interest payments to the bank and the real estate taxes had been deductible from federal income tax, and during the 1960s, because his income had been going up, the veteran had begun taking itemized deductions on his tax returns. That's suburban real estate, which has been going up in value steadily for 20 years.

It's a rare householder who has owned a house for more than, say, five years (which allows time for price increases to absorb the broker's commission and closing costs) who wouldn't find when he goes to sell it that he's come out ahead of the game.

From an economist's point of view, of course, this is a naive way to look at the game, because the homeowner could have put his money into stocks instead of the house and *perhaps* come out even further ahead. But this is, in fact, the game most people play, and they're not necessarily wrong—after all, while the money was in the market, they'd have had to live somewhere.

In recent years, on the crude, non-economist's reckoning, many people have wound up ahead of the game—or broken even—when they borrowed money to buy a car. Take, for example, a department-store assistant buyer in Dallas, making about $12,000 a year, who in 1967 bought a $3,000 Pontiac, putting down $750 and using a two-year installment loan for the other $2,250. His monthly payments were $108, including the cost of a term life-insurance policy that guaranteed that his family would own the car and not owe any money even if he died before the installment loan was paid. That brought his total cost to $3,342. If he had come around with $3,342 to his Pontiac dealer in 1969, he probably could not have bought as good a car for the money: automobile prices had gone up 11% in those two years.

More than that: between 1967 and 1969, the buyer's income had risen from $12,000 to $13,500. The $108 monthly payment he made the month after he bought the car represented 9% of his pre-tax income, but by the time he made the last payment it represented less than 8% of his pre-tax income. The burden of carrying the car had steadily eased over the life of the loan.

Should he have done without?

One can object that if he had done without and saved his money until he could pay cash he would have had a new car rather than a two-year-old car in 1969. But he had enjoyed the use of the car for two years, and now that he has finished his monthly payments he has reopened the possibility of using credit to buy anything he wishes—even another new car if he wants one. The inclusion of the term life or disability insurance policies in the loan agreement, one of the really bright ideas of recent years, means that being in debt for a car will probably *never* catch up with his family, even if he dies or has a serious illness; he is, of course, vulnerable to a depression that leaves him unemployed.

Good times for a borrower

During periods of prosperity and inflation, from the point of view of the borrower, the credit machinery works like a watch. Because prices are going up, waiting to buy something for cash means you have to pay more for it when you do buy it—which means that the interest you pay on a loan you take to buy now is really a lot less than it looks. Because wages are going up, the burden of repayment gets a little lighter all the time. And because the economy is booming, the breadwinner can moonlight a little, or his wife can take a part-time or even a full-time job if it turns out something extra is needed to pay the bills. But the economy can turn down, too, and as the engineers at Boeing have learned the hard way, most of the things that work in your favor on the way up turn against you when there's trouble.

Again, it's important to know what you're doing—to borrow when you see overtime opportunities or a promotion ahead, not when you fear hard times; to maintain credit for the

things the family needs by using it only spar-
ingly for luxuries; to measure the cost of borrowing against the value received from buying.

═══════════════════════════════════════

It's interesting to note that people do follow this
rule: during the recession from June 1970 through
February of 1971, there was very little change in the
volume of consumer credit outstanding. But when
the economy began turning up in the spring of 1971,
borrowing rose quickly. A record for new credit in a
single month was set in November of that year, when
Americans added $1.266 billion in consumer debt.

Your situation must be the key to your decision.
It's wise to buy something you need that's on sale,
or to get the right bridge made to end that toothache
forever, even if you have to borrow for the purpose.
But it's folly to borrow just to buy something pretty
in the window.

CHAPTER III

What Money Costs:

1. When the Lender Is Worried

People borrow money to buy things or do things; people lend money to make money. These two kinds of people come together in what economists call "credit markets," though there aren't any market places you can find and visit. And even to the economist, the credit markets are made up of quite a large number of smaller markets, all influencing each other.

There are many different kinds of loans, each with its own average interest rate, which will vary to some extent from state to state and may change from day to day. Sometimes you can borrow at an interest rate on the low side for the kind of loan you take, but the way to control the costs of your borrowing is to make sure your loan is in the lowest-priced category of loan you can qualify to receive.

In general, the interest charges on a loan—the price of the money—will relate to how certain the lender can be that he will get his money back. An

At the very bottom of the ladder, there are people who can borrow money only from guys who talk out of the corner of their mouths, but who know how to figure interest at horrendous rates.

unmarried dishwasher living in a New York rooming house will find it almost impossible to borrow money at all, except from illegal loan sharks, because the lender is afraid the borrower will just melt away. An aristocratic diplomat accredited to the United Nations in the same city and living in a luxury furnished apartment may have even more trouble than the dishwasher. Not only can he disappear to his home country without any notice to his creditors, he can renege without being sued even if he stays in New York, because he has diplomatic immunity. If either of these gentlemen finds it urgent to borrow money, he will probably have to go to a pawnbroker and put up as "collateral" for the loan some valuable personal possession like a watch or a musical instrument which will have to be worth about three times what the pawnbroker will lend him; and then he will have to pay interest at a rate up to 42% a year on whatever he borrows. (The diplomat could do better if he had U.S. securities to put up as collateral.)

That's the worst case.

The garnishment of a logger

The next-to-worst is the logger in the Oregon woods. His employment tends to be seasonal, and his occupation is one in which, by tradition, when a man gets some money he runs through it. Worse yet, he is borrowing money in a state which has the highest rate of personal bankruptcy of any.

One reason for the high rate of personal bankruptcy is a law which allows a lender to "garnishee," take directly from an employer, part of a worker's wages if he has failed to pay back a loan. If a man has overloaded himself with debts, and all his creditors rush to garnishee his wages at the same time, he has no out except bankruptcy. But if the logger has been repeatedly employed by the same lumber company and pays rent on the same place in town all year long, a personal loan company may decide he's a reasonable risk. But it's still a real risk from the loan company's point of view—no security, and a borrower who's off in the woods half the year—and the interest rate could be as high as 40% a year.

Lending borrowed money

Personal loan companies are always an expensive source of money. They have to be, if you think about it, because in most cases what they lend you is money they borrowed—they have to make their profit on top of the interest rates *they* pay. Other lenders will always charge less.

As a general rule, if the only place you *can* borrow is a loan company, you'd better think hard about whether you really *need* whatever it is you're borrowing to buy or do.

On the next step along the risk ladder we find a young housewife in a suburb of Minneapolis, whose baby sister is getting married three weeks from Saturday. The $350 Givenchy gown she sees at Dayton's is exactly right for her to wear to the wedding.

A worrisome young housewife

Now, the store is delighted to see her and to make the sale on credit, but at the same time she *is* just a little worrisome. If she's splurging all over the place,

The dress is a dream—and a dream of a buy. Nothing down, months and months to pay, but the department store revolving credit charge is heavy.

it may be a long time before she wants to pay for the dress. The store can't get its money back by repossessing and reselling the dress, because used clothing isn't worth much. She is not, of course, in the same class as the transient dishwasher in the rooming house. The lady has a husband who makes $285 a week, they have a house and a nursery-age child and a baby, and the money can be found, somehow, someday, to pay the bills. But going to court to make her pay would be expensive and bad publicity.

The credit revolves and revolves

Department stores like Dayton's and mail-order houses (like Sears and Spiegel and Montgomery Ward) and others who sell at retail (like gasoline companies) run special credit systems to help customers buy things they can't afford right now. The basic system is the "revolving credit" plan, which allows you to buy at stores (separately at each store, sometimes with unfortunate results) goods up to a certain maximum value, usually $300 or $500 for the household. At the start of each month, the store sends a statement which tells you your current balance, the interest you now owe on that balance (calculated by law, in most states, at a maximum figure of 1½% per month, which means 18% a year), and the minimum payment you are required to make (usually one-twelfth of the balance-plus-interest). By paying more than the required minimum, you reduce your interest charges for next month, and increase your capacity to borrow at the store for new purchases.

In many states, the 1½ % maximum interest charge is reduced to 1% for balances over $500, which means that many stores will refuse to extend more than $500 credit on a revolving plan. But some will allow you to set a higher limit on yourself, if your income and what you want to do with the money (e.g., buy new kitchen equipment) make sense.

Paying for those who don't pay

That's a high interest rate, 18%. Small loan company rates are higher still, and pawnbroker rates are gigantic. These rates are high in part because they have to cover not only the usual cost of money but also the repayment of principal and interest on the loans which people never pay back at all.

It's easier to get credit from stores and loan companies than from banks, but for that reason they're more likely to lend to people who just can't make it—and everyone who borrows from them pays for that fact.

In a way, it's very unfair: in many cases, it's a part of the burden of being poor, because it applies a penalty to all members of a class, whether they individually deserve that penalty or not. Think of the uproar that would follow if the government analyzed income tax returns by likelihood of attempts to cheat, and then assessed a surtax on everybody with an income over a certain figure because the rich are more likely to cheat on their taxes than the poor are. That would be an exact parallel to what happens when poor people borrow money.

Using a department-store or mail-order revolving credit plan may make sense when the borrowing allows you to buy something on sale that you would otherwise buy at a considerably higher price later in the year. A $100 suit or dress paid for through a year's installments on a revolving credit plan will cost about $110, which is fine if it is a $130 suit marked down. Otherwise, it's a very expensive way to shop.

The rates that never go down

Nearly all states set maximum interest rates that may be charged. (For the maximum in your state, see the table in Chapter XIII.) Loan company rates range from 36% on the first $30 down to 18% on amounts above $1,000. For department stores the figure is typically 18%, though some states allow a slightly higher charge for revolving credit when the amount borrowed is small. And in many states, the loan company is "restricted" to 30%. These laws are unquestionably necessary to protect poor borrowers. Unfortunately, they tend to become the minimum figure as well as the maximum figure: whatever happens to all the other interest rates for all the other kinds of loans, loan company and revolving credit rates seem to stay the same.

The law that has made the most difference to small borrowers in recent years is the federal Truth in Lending Act of 1968, which doesn't do anything to control rates but forces all lenders to tell you, as a simple percentage, the price you're paying for services and the money.

The Truth in Lending Act is referred to throughout this book; more details as well as sample forms required by it are given in Chapter XIII.

CHAPTER IV

What Money Costs:

2. When Everything Is Routine

Two-thirds of all new cars in the U.S. are bought on an installment plan; at any one time there will be $30 billion of credit outstanding to help people buy cars. With that much money to be loaned, there are obviously lots of lenders in the business.

The easiest one to deal with—no trouble at all —is the automobile dealer himself. Except that the dealer is not really the lender. He acts as agent for somebody else—for the credit company associated with the auto manufacturer whose cars he sells (GM, Chrysler, and Ford have their own); for the local bank or finance company (which is probably "floor planning" his inventory, that is, lending him the money that allows him to stock the cars he sells); or for a small loan company (like Household Finance, Beneficial Finance, and Seaboard Finance) which will probably pay him a portion of the service charge on every installment contract he writes for them. The dealer may very possibly have in his desk as good a credit deal as you can get anywhere, but that may not be the deal he first offers you.

The best financing arrangement a dealer
may have to offer the purchaser of a new car
may not be the first one he takes out of his desk.

Never buy a car on a dealer-proposed installment contract until you have checked to see
what kind of auto loan you can get directly
from a bank.

Banks got into the consumer-loan business only
after World War II, and many people still feel the
banks don't really want their business despite a near-
orgy of television advertising about how friendly
everybody is over at The Old First Trust. And it's still
true that many banks don't really want to make small
unsecured personal loans—but nearly all of them are
eager for auto loans. The amounts of money involved
are reasonably large, often over $2,000, which means
that their profits aren't eaten up by the costs of
paperwork. (The credit check, the loan agreement,
the internal memos and bookkeeping are all pretty
much the same for big and small loans.) While loans
to businesses can rarely be made to good credit customers at rates much above 8%, interest rates on auto
loans rarely fall below 11%. And the down payment
of one-quarter to one-third of the purchase price
(usually represented by the trade-in) frequently
covers the short-term depreciation of the car, which
means that any time the borrower stops paying, the
bank can repossess the car, sell it on a well-estab-
lished used-car market, and limit (to a very low figure)
or wipe out any loss on the loan—which is more than

can be said for some business loans the bank makes.

The department store buyer in Dallas, who came out ahead of the game, had a bank loan to buy his car. The "carrying charges," you will recall, added $342 to the price of a $3,000 car, over two years. Though it doesn't look like much, the interest rate on that loan works out to something just over 14½%.

Figuring the true interest rate

Here is how that is calculated: The formula for figuring annual interest rate is

$$\text{Rate} = \frac{2 \times P \times C}{A \times (N + 1)}$$

P = number of payment periods
    in one year   = 12
C = carrying charges   = $342.00
A = amount of the loan   = $2250.00
N = the total number of installments   = 24

Here is the arithmetic:

$$\frac{2 \times 12 \times \$342.00}{\$2250.00 \times (24 + 1)} = \frac{\$8208.00}{56250.00} = .146 \text{ or } 14\frac{1}{2}\%$$

That 15% is not all "interest rate"—it includes the term life insurance which guarantees that the bank is repaid and that payments on the car would not burden the buyer's wife if he died before the family owned the car free and clear, plus various costs associated with closing and processing a contract.

But from the buyer's point of view it's all the cost of the money (he wouldn't need the insurance policy if he didn't owe on the car). Yet even at 15%, the car buyer came out ahead of the game—in an inflationary period.

Live here, borrow there

Longer loans mean higher total interest charges, and probably higher interest rates. On a 36-month loan, the Dallas car buyer's Pontiac would have cost him $3,630, almost $300 more. Smaller down payments also tend to raise the rate the buyer must pay as well as raising the total interest cost because interest has to be paid on that much more loan.

Quite apart from these common-sense rules, auto loans are not necessarily the same from bank to bank, and it may be worth looking in on two or three before deciding. You can borrow money in the city for a purchase in the suburbs, and vice versa—and sometimes the suburban bank can offer a lower interest rate, because it doesn't have to pay high rents and it probably has fewer established corporate customers, which means greater desire for business like auto loans.

Don't beef about your lemon to the manager
of the bank or finance company that bought
your promissory note from the dealer. He couldn't
care less. Any defects in the car
are not his responsibility, and you still
have to make the installment payments.

In January of 1972 some banks in the New York City area were making auto loans at just under 10% and others were charging just over 11%. Some years ago, the mathematics of comparing what different banks were offering would have been a chore, but the Truth in Lending Act takes care of that. Now the automobile dealer and the banks have to tell you, in the simplest terms, what it is they're charging, the total cost of the loan and the breakdown, so much for interest, so much for insurance, so much for closing costs, etc. The opposite page shows what the relevant segment of the promissory note might look like.

1. AMOUNT OF CREDIT $_____
   (includes Net Balance due on any previous obligation
   $_____)

2. OTHER CHARGES
   (Not part of finance charge)

	A To Be Paid in Cash	B To Be Financed
FEES		
Registration	$_____	$_____
Filing	$_____	$_____
Recording	$_____	$_____
License	$_____	$_____
Other	$_____	$_____
INSURANCE		
Property	$_____	$_____
Liability	$_____	$_____
Credit Life	$_____	$_____
Credit Life & Disability	$_____	$_____
Other	$_____	$_____
Total other charges to be financed (Col. B)		$_____

3. Sub Total (1 + 2B) $_____

4. Deduct Prepaid Finance Charge (6B) $_____

5. Amount Financed (3 − 4) $_____

6. FINANCE CHARGE
   A. Interest Computed on Item 3
      (or min. charge $_____) $_____
      _____ $_____
   B. Prepaid Finance Charge $_____
      (Itemize) $_____
   FINANCE CHARGE (total of A + B) $_____

7. ANNUAL PERCENTAGE RATE
                                        _____%

8. TOTAL OF PAYMENTS   (5 + 6A) $_____

Whether you borrow from the dealer or the bank, by the way, you wind up owing the bank or the credit company with which the dealer has his arrangement. The dealer simply "assigns" your loan to a lending institution, which in return immediately pays him the cash for the car.

If there's anything wrong with the car, you have to keep paying anyway, as the law now stands in most states. The bank or other lending institution is a "holder in due course," with no responsibility for the quality of what you bought when you incurred the debt.

This law has now been changed in New York, New Jersey, and other states to free borrowers from the need to keep paying back loans when the item purchased with the loan doesn't work properly; you might let your state legislators know you support this law in your state. The neighborhood legal offices opened under the poverty program have eased the defective merchandise problem a little by making it possible for poor people to sue a storekeeper if the store sues them.

One of the few advantages the department store revolving-credit system has over the auto loan is that you are billed by the department store rather than by a bank. If the washing machine doesn't work or the overcoat arrives with a button torn off, the store *may* hold off on dunning you for your payments while the complaints department investigates your claim that the merchandise is defective. Stores accept returns; auto dealers usually don't.

One source of credit for auto loans may be even cheaper than the bank: a credit union where you work.

Credit unions go back to the time before the banks made personal loans, and they were a grand invention, a way for workers to invest their savings to help each other. In effect, a credit union is a mutual savings bank with both depositors and borrowers limited to members of the union. It pays interest to members (usually the same interest as the local savings bank) on the money deposited, and charges interest on the money loaned. Because there is rarely any need to do any investigating of applicants for loans, credit unions save some of a banker's costs off the top. They also don't have to pay for all those glass walls and marble counters, and except for a small rainy-day fund they're not expected to make a profit.

Most credit unions are state-chartered, and are operated in a single factory or for the employees of a city or a department store. But there are also worldwide credit unions, like the one at the Associated

Press, which can be used by employees of that news service anywhere, and a number of very large federally-chartered credit unions in the government bureaus, of which the biggest is probably that of the Postal Service. Ethnic and social groups and some religious groups (like the Ukrainian Orthodox Church) may have their own credit unions.

A credit union at the place you work is a good
source of low-interest loans. One reason:
they have austere working quarters rather than
the posh offices that banks flaunt.

Rates vary from credit union to credit union. Personal loans tend to be like savings bank passbook loans, which we'll consider presently: people borrow back what they've deposited, paying ¾ of 1% per month for the privilege of using their own money (and the protection of a term life insurance and/or disability policy, *not* offered in most savings bank passbook loans, to guarantee that if the borrower dies or becomes too disabled to work while he owes money his family's savings will be secure). Automobile loans seem to be the largest category, and these are made to members of the credit union much as banks make them to people who walk in the door: at 1% a month by large credit unions, including the term insurance. This term insurance, by the way, is very inexpensive on a group basis, and adds less than 1% a year (on the average balance) to the cost of the loan—in the example of the Dallas buyer, something like $20. The protection is easily worth the price.

Vacation for the dentist

Both banks and credit unions will make unsecured personal loans for any legitimate purpose to a regularly employed person. Many people have borrowed for vacation travel: for example, a Japanese-American dentist working for a health plan in San Francisco, who wanted to take his wife and two daughters to see an Old Country he had never, in fact, seen himself. This was going to be an expensive trip. Including the stopover in Hawaii, the three weeks would run a thousand dollars for each person, maybe a little more. The dentist had $2,500 saved for the trip; the credit union at the health plan loaned him the remaining $1,500, with a year to repay in monthly installments, at a finance charge of only $93 (1% per month on the balance outstanding each month)—again including the price of term insurance.

For an employed dentist the cost of a one-year $1,500 loan at a California bank in 1971 would have been $100, or about a percentage point higher.

CHAPTER V

What Money Costs:

3. When the Lender Feels Secure

Consider now the case of a successful real-estate salesman in Cincinnati, whose son is in college. Once upon a time—within the memory of men not yet fifty —it was possible for boys and girls to "work their way through college," but no more, not by a big margin. Today, in fact, a man earning $20,000 a year before taxes probably can't put his children through college out of current income. The salesman himself went to a private college, is a loyal alumnus, and has always wanted his son to follow in his footsteps. Private colleges as a matter of principle won't give scholarships to the sons and daughters of men earning $20,000 a year. In addition to whatever money the boy will be able to make in summer jobs and part-time work while he studies, his father will have to put up about $2,000 a year for the next four years.

(There are a variety of long-term, low-interest federal, state and private loans available for students. The types of loans and availabilities vary from state to state: some loans require parents as co-signers; others allow 18-year-old students to accept full responsibility for the loan. But our salesman didn't want his son to

Higher education has so much higher a price tag on it these days that parents who make too much money to allow their children to qualify for scholarships—but not enough to have *that* much money lying around—have to borrow to finance a college education.

start out in life with a debt to pay, no matter how easy the repayment conditions.)

The high cost of a college education is not news to our salesman, of course, though the actual figures have come as a bit of a shock. He has been a careful provider for his family through the years; he has savings accounts and life insurance policies, he owns some stock in blue-chip companies, and he has paid off most of the mortgage on his house. He therefore has four sources of loans, from institutions that know for a fact they will get their money back.

Of the four sources, the cheapest is undoubtedly the life insurance company.

Every life insurance policy except a term policy has a cash value, representing the money already paid in and that fraction of the earnings on the money the company has retained as its guarantee that the total average cash in the policies will be enough to pay off the death benefits that every policy will eventually have to pay to the heirs of the insured. Life-insurance companies invest very conservatively (in most states they must, by law), and to meet their investment target they need net earnings of something less than 5% a year. They are thus willing to lend money to their policy-holders, up to 95% of the cash value of the policy, for only 5% or 5½% a year, though there are cases where the rate has risen to 6%.

The loan from the life insurance company, of course, reduces the benefits the salesman's family would receive if he died before paying it back. And because this isn't an installment loan—he will pay it on his own time, when he's ready—the salesman does run the risk of *permanently* reducing his life insurance coverage. But, after all, part of the purpose of buying the life insurance was to guarantee a good future for the kids, and using some of the money now to pay college bills meets the same purpose.

The psychology of borrowing vs. saving

The second source available to our salesman is borrowing from a savings bank against the money in his own account there. This looks like borrowing

A life insurance policy (if it is not term insurance) provides the cheapest method of taking out a loan.

your own money and paying for the privilege, and that's just what it is. But somehow, people find it psychologically much easier to pay back a loan every month than to build up a savings account. And the *net* cost of the loan (the interest you have to pay the bank less the interest the bank pays you on your savings) will run only about 1%. At New York's Bowery Savings Bank, the nation's largest, the rate for passbook loans at the end of 1971 was 6.3% on the average balance for a one-year loan, as against passbook earnings of 5%. That means a $1,000 loan carries an interest charge of $34.75 (remember, your *average* loan over the course of the year is only a little more than half the total loaned to you at the start, because you keep paying it off.) As against that, the interest earned on the average balance pledged against the loan (which keeps going down as you pay it off) runs just under $28.

The actual out-of-pocket cost of the $1,000 one-year passbook loan at these rates is only about $7—and if you're in a 30% tax bracket and itemize deductions, the real cost is only about $5.

You pay that $5 strictly to protect you from your own weakness, but for many people it's probably wiser to admit weakness and pay a regular monthly installment than to strip themselves of their savings and try to force themselves to start all over again. In fact, our salesman doesn't like to think of himself as weak, and he won't borrow at his savings bank, but many people do.

Our salesman has a third source of loan money available to him because he owns stock. Borrowing against the value of stock certificates deposited as collateral for the loan is like borrowing against a savings account passbook, but it can make more sense to the strong-willed. Selling a stock now to buy it back later looks bad if the price goes from 20 to 40 before you return to the market. (Of course, it could also go from 20 to 10.) If you think the stock is under-priced and will rise, borrowing against its value makes

The would-be borrower who owns securities, particularly those considered "blue-chip," is in a position to get credit on favorable conditions. He needs merely to pledge his securities as collateral, and pay a low interest rate.

sense. Moreover, while it usually costs nothing to take money out of a savings bank and put it back (there may be some loss of interest payments for a quarter depending on the kind of account), buying and selling stocks requires the payment of a broker's commission on both ends, likely to be as much as 3% of the money involved (counting both purchase and sale) on small transactions. If the loan is to run less than a year, and you think you want to hold on to that stock, it will almost always make sense to borrow against securities rather than to sell them.

Interest will be determined by general interest rates in the economy (at the end of 1971 loans secured by stocks were being made at rates from 5¼% to 7%) but it will always be low compared to the interest on a personal loan or an auto loan. And you keep the dividends on the stock.

For various reasons connected with stock market crashes of the past, the bank isn't permitted to lend much more than half the current market value of a stock, and if the stock price drops dramatically you may be called on to prepay some of the loan or put up more collateral and keep the bank protected. But this sort of collateral loan ought to be taken more often than it is.

Interest costs on a personal loan fully secured by the pledge of securities will run less than half the costs of borrowing on a department store revolving credit plan. There's no loss of control; any time you want to sell the stock you can tell the bank to do it for you, cancel out your loan, and pay you whatever is left.

A Wall Street plunger looking forward to a good year bought his wife for her birthday a $1,200 combination color-television-and-stereo system. On department store credit, which he could have arranged, the interest cost of buying the machine on time would have run about $100; by borrowing at a bank against securities he planned to hold anyway, the investor saved $50. There are lots of people on Wall Street who scoff at saving $50, but some of the successful ones don't—and that's among the reasons why they're successful.

Back to our salesman: is a loan based on securities as collateral the right one for him? No, because he needs to borrow for a long term.

For long-term loans, pledging securities rather than selling them is much less likely to be profitable: the average dividend yield has been running well under 4% and on a long-term loan you won't be able to borrow for less than 7%.

***

Our salesman is in a situation where he isn't likely to repay the college loan entirely for some time. The idea of borrowing against the security of his blue-chip stocks, while briefly appealing, doesn't stand up on second thought.

The drawbacks to increasing the mortgage

A final option: increasing the mortgage on the house. This will cost the salesman considerably more than either a loan from the insurance company or a passbook loan against savings. When you deal with your insurance company or your bank you are operating in a context of a continuing relationship— you're not just somebody who wants to borrow money, you're a regular customer.

***

Increasing the mortgage will probably cost more than the loan against securities, because it's a more cumbersome procedure, perhaps involving writing a new mortgage, increasing the amount of the loan on an "open-end" mortgage (allowed only in some states) or acquiring a second mortgage at substantially higher rates.

Like the loan secured by stock certificates, it will carry an interest rate that can't be predicted much in advance: mortgages are in the economists' "credit market" for real. The bank has to judge your application for a loan on real property against all the other applications that come in for similar loans, and you have to pay the same rate everybody else is paying. So we must temporarily leave our salesman pondering his course of action, and look into the way interest rates are set and how mortgages work before we can learn how he will decide to finance his son's college expenses.

CHAPTER VI

How Interest Rates Are Set

When we talk about interest rates, we are talking about the price for money. Money is a commodity, like copper or leather or rice—only different. Because, when you cut right through all the layers of stock exchanges and bonds and banks and loan companies, nobody can produce money but the government. And because price is the result of interaction between buyers and sellers, the government as the only seller has a lot to say about how high the interest rate stands.

You might think that if the Defense Department needs another billion dollars for big airplanes, the

President could just tell the Mint to print up a billion dollars. But one of the things the Congress has always been careful about is its control on how the President gets money. Back in the 19th century, except for a few years during and after the Civil War (when Lincoln was empowered to print paper money, and turned out about $400,000,000 of the first "greenbacks"), American currency was in gold pieces and bank notes issued by nationally chartered banks. The banks were expected to keep some gold reserve behind them.

Creating currency

Since 1913, the currency supply has been effectively in the hands of the Federal Reserve System, and more than 99% of all the paper money in circulation in the United States exists because it was ordered from the Bureau of Printing and Engraving by the Federal Reserve System. (Until the mid-1960s, the Treasury still issued one-dollar "silver certificates" which were "payable to the bearer in silver on demand," but the price of silver got so high it was decided to make the Federal Reserve System the guarantor of the one-dollar bills as well as of the larger denominations.) The result is that money is never printed by Executive Order, but only on demand by the Federal Reserve System. The Fed, as it is known to its friends, is an independent agency of the government, with a Board of Governors appointed by the President and confirmed by the Senate for terms of 14 years, which insulates them pretty thoroughly from political pressure.

As of the start of 1972, the currency in circulation in the United States ran a total of about $90 billion. (About a third of that total was in $20 bills, by the way; about a tenth of it was in *coins*—think of all those coins!) Another $140 billion was "circulating" in the form of bank accounts in commercial banks, which are money just as much as the green-and-gray printed bills are, because checks drawn on such accounts will be almost equally acceptable as payment for goods and services.

Most of the bank-account money at any given moment has been created by the banks. In doing so they rely on the cheering fact that not everybody comes around at the same time to take cash for his deposits.

Let's say you deposit $2,000 in a checking account. The bank then lends $3,000 to your neighbor to buy a car, in effect creating a $3,000 deposit for him, which is transferred to the account of the automobile dealer. Now the bank has $5,000 of obligations, against which it can place your $2,000 cash deposit and your neighbor's $3,000 I.O.U. Obviously, if you and the automobile dealer both come around for your money at the same time, the bank won't have it. But in fact, as was proved by the earliest merchant

The banker takes—for a consideration; and
lends—for a consideration. It is
possible for everyone to profit in a deal like this,
but not necessarily equally.

bankers in Europe four hundred years ago, you and
the dealer (multiplied by the enormous number of
such transactions in even any one bank) *won't* need
cash at the same time. If you do, the bank can sell
("discount") the borrower's note for the cash its customers demand.

The system works very well most of the time, with
other banks or private investors in the credit market
willing to buy the borrower's note if the banks puts
it up for sale. But sometimes the system breaks down.
One of the things the government learned in the late

19th century is that the country couldn't risk leaving the production of the money supply entirely in private hands. In 1907, there was a nationwide depression, recalled today as a "money panic," caused almost entirely because all the banks got scared at once, called in all the loans that they could, wouldn't renew others that came due, and tried to sell all their borrowers' notes in the shrinking market.

How the Fed exercises control

There are some economists who believe that the Great Depression of 1929–33 was caused by failure to handle the money supply correctly. By then, however, control of these matters was in the hands of the Federal Reserve System, which had been created in the aftermath of the Panic of 1907.

The Fed controls what the banks do about creating money. First, the Fed decides what proportion of its *total* deposits (money left on account *plus* money created by loans) each bank must keep as a "reserve" in cash or in its own deposits in the Fed itself.

Usually, this "reserve requirement" is about 25% for big city banks, less for country banks. That's a gross control of how much money can be in the system.

Second, the Fed itself buys borrowers' notes from banks that need more reserves to stay within these requirements. These are really loans to the banks by the Fed. The interest rate the Fed charges to the banks for these loans—technically, the "rediscount rate"—in effect puts a floor under the interest rate the banks can charge their new customers and greatly influences the ceiling, the top rate the banks will ask.

The Fed can turn up or down the flow of money, and thus control the amount of credit available as well as the level of interest charges.

If the interest rate charged to customers gets very far above the Fed's rediscount rate, it becomes profitable for more and more banks to borrow extra reserves from the Fed and make more loans.

This increases the supply of money, and an increased supply of any commodity will, of course, tend to drive down its price.

The final weapon of the Fed is more subtle. The greatest reservoir of locked-up money in the United States—like gold in the mattresses of French farmers —is the huge volume of government bonds.

Getting the gold out of the mattresses

The U.S. bonds most people buy with payroll deductions and the like are not salable—you have to cash them in. But most government bonds, sold in large denominations to businesses and banks, trade in a bond market just like ordinary corporate bonds. (Some of these marketable government bonds are bought by individuals, usually through their banks, in $1,000 denominations; in 1969, when interest rates on these short-term government bonds got as high as 8%, many ordinary people came into this previously professional market.)

The Fed has the power to buy and sell government bonds. When the Fed goes into the "open market" and buys bonds, it pumps additional money, and thus additional reserves, into the banking system. It's just as though a lot of French peasants suddenly put their gold into the local banks instead of into the mattress. When the Fed sells government bonds, taking in cash from the banks and the public, it draws money and thus reserves out of the banking system.

Because this sort of action is reversible overnight, and can be done without any publicity, it is the Fed's favorite way of working, especially at those seasons (tax time, Christmas, etc.) when the banks regularly need more money.

No one gives orders to the Fed

Incidentally, the Fed is remarkably free to make these technical decisions on technical grounds, without interference from the rest of the government. It took a long time to win that freedom, because what the Fed does indirectly controls not only the interest rates the banks charge for loans, but also the interest rate the government itself must pay on the national debt. In the late 1940s, having piled up during World

War II a much larger national debt than anybody had ever expected to see, the government demanded that the Fed use its powers to keep interest rates low. The Fed fought back, insisting that interest rates could be kept low during an economic boom (when every business was demanding money to expand, every customer was demanding money to buy) only by flooding the country with bank credit, which would cheapen the value of money itself, creating an explosively destructive inflation. Very reluctantly—and even today the federal Treasury has moments when it would love to order the Fed around—the government decided to let the Fed handle problems of money supply, even if it meant higher interest costs burdening the annual federal budget.

The interest rate the government has to pay on new government bonds is the foundation on which all other interest rates rest. For obvious reasons: no loan can be safer than a loan to the government.

Above that, other loans command higher interest, depending on the degree of safety, the costs per dollar in making the loan, and the length of time before the loan is paid back.

The market for long-term money and the market for short-term money tend to be somewhat separate. In theory, long-term loans should always carry higher interest rates than short-term loans. In fact, because insurance companies and pension funds need to make long-term investments to guarantee their long-term needs, there is a steady supply of funds for long-term loans, which holds down their interest rates even when rates for short-term borrowing go sky high.

Bumping the ceiling

If the interest rate on government bonds and the rediscount rate at the Fed go up, the interest on all loans to businesses and on most consumer loans will also go up. (Some consumer loans made by personal loan companies and department stores are already so high that the law won't let them go higher.) If the interest on government bonds and the rediscount rate go down, then the interest on almost all loans to people will go down.

The interest rate on any one loan is set at the time the loan is made. Fluctuations in the credit markets affect only *new* loans.

The Fed does not attempt to move interest rates up or down according to political or philosophical theories. The art of managing the money supply of a nation is to manipulate interest rates to reflect conditions in the economy. In boom times, the price of money should go up, making businessmen hesitate about expanding their inventories or building new plants and simultaneously making individuals reluctant to buy houses and cars. The net effect is to slow down what could otherwise develop into a runaway inflation. In depressed times, the price of money should go down, to encourage manufacturers to invest, retailers to stock their stores, and customers to buy. In recessions, money is about the only commodity for which prices (interest rates) do go down (because money costs almost nothing to make), but they would decline much more slowly than they do without the Fed standing in the background and pushing them downward.

The belief that there is going to be an inflation can keep interest rates high even during a recession, because lenders will be reluctant to lend money that will come back to them worth less than it is now.

Lenders don't *have* to lend. They can in many cases buy stocks or real estate or precious stones—anything that might go up in value if money goes down in value—instead of putting their savings at the disposal of the credit market. Moreover, when the economy seems to be dropping, the belief that there's going to be a depression may scare bankers enough to make them insist on being "liquid"—keeping money in government bonds or very short-term loans

—which prevents the necessary expansion of the money supply. The work of the Board of Governors of the Federal Reserve System, dealing with all these problems, would be very hard indeed, except that so few people know anything about the way the Fed works that even the newspapers are a little afraid to criticize.

What goes on inside the Fed is something
the Fed takes great pains to keep
from the public, usually with complete success.

Fluctuations in the money market are felt in all lending, but the borrower feels them more on long-term loans than on short-term ones. Two percent more on the auto loan to the department store buyer in Dallas would have added about $40 to the cost of his car. But a rise from 6% to 8% interest on a 30-year $25,000 mortgage on a house means—are you ready? —*more than $12,000 additional interest cost* on the house.

Elsewhere in this series the subject of mortgages will be examined extensively and in depth. But the subject must be looked at here, too, because the mortgage loan is far and away the biggest loan any ordinary consumer will undertake in his life. So let's take a look at mortgages, the way the Cincinnati real estate salesman—who knows all about mortgages—would look at them in deciding how to finance his son's college education.

CHAPTER VII

Some Do's and Don't's about Mortgages

The word comes from the legal French the Normans brought to England in the 11th century. It means "dead hand," and it still has rather frightening connotations. We talk of people "mortgaging their future." And so long as it was a loan with a fixed term that had to be paid off or renewed at the end of the term, a mortgage was indeed scary. Anyone who had a mortgage on his house or his farm was at the mercy of conditions in the credit market when the mortgage came due. If he was unlucky just in the timing, his interest rate could soar; if the date fell at a time of a money panic, he could lose his property simply because he could not find anyone willing to lend. It was luck: no justice in it at all. Lots of farmers did lose their farms in the 1920s and 1930s, just that way.

And one couldn't always blame the lenders. The value of houses and farm buildings can deteriorate. Between 1929 and 1933 especially, the value of any mortgaged property fell so far that it was unreasonable to ask a lender to renew the old mortgage without a considerable reduction in the size of the loan—at a time when very few farmers had the cash to pay back any part of a mortgage. The situation got so bad that the state of Minnesota passed a law forcing mortgage-holders to renew their loans, and the U.S. Supreme Court upheld it, Constitution or no Constitution.

From fear to rejoicing

The answer to this recurring problem was found in the 1930s, with the self-amortizing mortgage and a government guarantee (on certain classes of houses and farms and for certain borrowers, like veterans) that the mortgage would eventually be paid. Instead of paying only the interest and renewing the loan each time it came due, the householder would make a monthly payment large enough to cover both interest charges and the complete repayment of the loan over the life of the mortgage. The day when the mortgage ended had been a day of fear and trembling; these new arrangements made it a day of rejoicing.

Mortgages are different from other loans. Though they are personal obligations of the borrower, the lender is much more concerned about the piece of property against which the mortgage lies than about the character and quality of the people who borrow the money. The security is the land and the house, not the future income of their owner.

Unlike a personal loan, a mortgage loan is granted on the value of the property rather than on the reliability of the applicant.

Where the auto loan comes with a term life insurance policy, the mortgage loan requires the borrower to maintain fire insurance on the building.

Most mortgages come from lenders who are not in the short-term personal loan business. Personal loan, auto loan, and department store revolving credit money is usually money created by banks. Most mortgage money comes from other people's savings, invested in life-insurance policies or savings and loan associations or savings banks. These are, of course, the right sources for long-term loans like mortgages, because most of the people who are putting the money into these institutions don't expect to be taking it out again for a long time.

Most of the payment is interest

The self-amortizing feature of the modern mortgage loan means that *total interest costs* are in reality higher than the simple *rate of interest* tells you, because most of the payments you make at the beginning go for interest charges.

If you take a loan of $25,000 at 6% and pay it off in 30 years on a self-amortizing basis, you will pay just under $1,900 a year in equal monthly or quarterly payments every year over the entire life of the loan. Your early payments are nearly all interest, and the principal goes down very slowly. After 15 years, you will still owe $17,500. And your total interest cost will be about $29,000.

But if you take a "declining balance" mortgage with a loan of $25,000 and pay off the principal in equal installments over 30 years, you owe about $12,500 after 15 years, at the midpoint of the loan. At 6% interest on the "declining balance" of the loan, total payments to the bank in the first year (principal-plus-interest) will run about $2,300; but after 15 years of paying off principal your annual payments are only about $1,600 a year—and in the last year of the loan you pay only about $860. The total interest cost is about $22,500.

In the early stages of the self-amortizing loan, a distressingly large hunk of the regular payments is eaten up by interest and only a tiny amount is applied to amortization of the principal.

On self-amortizing loans, as interest rates go up the proportion of the early payments that must go for interest also goes up. At 2% interest—to cite a dramatic but unreal situation—the difference between paying off principal in equal installments and paying on a self-amortizing basis is only about 12% extra cost for the self-amortizing loan—$7,500 against $8,400 for a $25,000, 30-year loan. (Of your first month's payment of $92.77, $41.66 goes for interest, $51.11 for amortization, or paying off the principal.) At 6% interest, as noted above, it's 28.4% more interest cost over the life of the mortgage—$22,500 as against $29,000. (Of your first month's payment of $149.90, $125 goes for interest, only $24.90 for amortization.)

Thus, rising interest rates penalize borrowers of mortgage loans more than the interest numbers alone can tell.

The "equity" you have in your house, the amount of the principal of the mortgage you have in fact paid off, is likely in the early years to be considerably less than you think. (The last chapter gives examples in tabular form.) At 6% on a self-amortizing mortgage of $25,000, for example, the $8,900 or so that you pay the bank during the first five years pays off only about

$1,700 of the principal of the loan. The self-amortizing mortgage, a brilliant socioeconomic invention that has saved many Americans from financial disaster, was more valuable from the 1930s through the 1950s, when interest rates were low, than it was in the late 1960s, when they climbed nearly out of sight.

Paying $41,000 for $25,000

An 8% 30-year self-amortizing mortgage, which was common in 1969 and 1970, makes the home buyer pay $41,000 for having borrowed $25,000. (Of the first month's payment of $183.45, $166.67 is interest and $16.78 amortization.)

Interest adds much more to the cost of a house than all the much-publicized wage increases the construction workers have been getting.

According to the National Association of Home Builders, on-site labor costs represented only 18% of the cost of a $30,000 home in 1969, and probably less than 20% in 1971. It was the interest rates, not the costs of construction, that made it so nearly impossible for middle-income Americans to buy their homes in the early 1970s. Fortunately, interest rates started down again after 1970 toward more sensible levels, and if we are lucky, they will stay down. Because interest rates were dropping in 1971, the monthly mortgage payments required of many new home buyers in early 1972 dropped slightly as compared with the previous years, even though the costs of land and building continued to go up.

There are ways to save a little money—though not much—in shopping for mortgages. The higher the down payment you are prepared to make, the lower the interest rate is likely to be on the rest, because the lender's risk is somewhat diminished—but we are talking here about reductions on the order of eighths of a percent. Sometimes, for the same reason of

When you shop for a mortgage, you should do exactly that:
shop around to see what rates you
are offered by the three principal sources
of mortgage money.

diminished risk, you can save something by using government-guaranteed mortgages—Veterans Administration for veterans, Federal Housing Administration for non-veterans. In the case of FHA usually the builder of the house has to qualify for an FHA mortgage, not the buyer; it's one of the selling points for a house. But an FHA mortgage includes ½% for the government (for insurance service), and most people take FHA mortgages to make the smallest possible down payment, which means higher interest costs despite the government guarantee. (There is no ½% charge on VA mortgages.) In general, commercial banks (which use the money in their savings departments for this purpose) and mutual savings banks charge somewhat lower interest rates on conventional mortgages though they will also demand somewhat higher down payments. Savings and loan associations tend to underwrite riskier mortgages, demand less down payment, and charge higher interest rates.

The best way to minimize mortgage costs is to buy a house only when interest rates are low. If you must buy when money is dear, shop for a clause that permits you to "refinance" the mortgage, pay it off ahead of time by taking a new mortgage for the purpose, when interest rates go down.

Different banks have different rules about this sort of thing. Some will not permit refinancing for the first three or five years, then allow prepayment without penalty at any time thereafter. Others charge a percentage of the balance—both 1% and ½% are common—as a penalty for prepayment. There are then, of course, the closing fees associated with the new mortgage to replace the old—perhaps as much as $200. But people who got stuck with an 8½% mortgage in 1970 will save all such costs in the first year of a new mortgage at 7%. If the old mortgage was for $25,000, for example, the amount saved would be 1½% of that sum, or $375, just in the first year.

A burden for your old age

Buyers over the age of forty might think hard about the advantages of the "declining balance" kind of mortgage referred to above, on which you pay off the principal in equal installments and your monthly or quarterly payment drops as the interest charge diminishes with the balance. That guarantees that the house won't be a burden to your old age, and allows you to build up a greater equity in it for possible future use. Some banks will write such mortgages only for commercial properties these days, but others will provide one for a home if you ask.

Our Cincinnati real estate salesman—the man we first met in Chapter V, pondering how to finance his son's college education—had bought his house in

1959, and was paying only 5½ % interest on his mortgage. In 1971 the house was worth considerably more than he had paid for it, and he could have taken a new mortgage that would give him all the cash he would need to help his son through all four years of college. But he would have had to increase the entire mortgage loan to 7½ %, greatly increasing his monthly mortgage burden now and forever.

Regretfully, the real estate salesman and his wife decided to pay the college bills by combining a life insurance loan with the gradual sale of some stocks and a cutback in their vacation plans.

CHAPTER VIII

How Much *Can* You Borrow?

Lenders investigate. Their first concern is whether or not you will pay back what you borrow, and to ease that concern they want to know where you live, where you work, how much you make, how much you already owe, and what your past record has been in paying your debts. Some of this information the lender will ask for directly—a sample application can be found in the appendix—some of it he'll go and find out for himself, usually by checking with a credit bureau. This is to some extent an invasion of your privacy—and this is part of the price you pay when you borrow money.

You can avoid this kind of question-and-answer session only if your loan will be "fully secured"—if it's a loan against a savings bank passbook or securities that will be deposited with the bank, or the cash value of a life insurance policy, or a mortgage on a house in which the down payment is large enough to assure the bank that if the mortgage has to be foreclosed the house can be sold for considerably more than the loan.

When you apply for an unsecured personal loan
you are naked to the lender, who puts you under
intensive scrutiny, personal as well as financial,
to assure himself that you are "good" for the money.

One criterion for how much you can borrow is this: how much do you have? The banker, being a businessman rather than a psychiatric social worker, often doesn't know and doesn't care whether a man of means who makes a fully secured loan is doing something foolish or not. But the man who does not have assets to pledge will have to give any lender a reason to believe that he's not borrowing so much money he will have trouble paying it back.

The most common rule of thumb allows loan officers at most banks to write loans calling for an average monthly payment of 10%, sometimes 13%, occasionally 15% of the borrower's take-home pay.

A great deal depends on the income of the borrower: If you're right on the edge of poverty, obviously you can't have much left over every month to pay installments; if you're over the average income for the area, you can probably squeeze out something extra to buy that bedroom set or color TV or pay the expenses connected with the new baby.

What's your track record?

There's also the question of your track record: if your salary is $195 a week and you just finished paying off a loan that took $91 a month, and you never

missed an installment, you'll have no trouble borrowing a thousand dollars from the bank. But if you've
been in trouble with past loans, if you have a history
of late payments, the bank is likely to suggest that you
were overstrained last time and ought not to do it
again. All these rule-of-thumb figures, of course, refer
to your *total* monthly payments on *all* indebtedness
except a mortgage, which usually counts as part of
your rent. If your housing costs for a mortgage and
real estate taxes run over 30% of your monthly income, though, the bank may worry about your ability
to handle installment debt, too.

The bigger your take-home paycheck, the bigger
the personal loan the lender will be inclined
to make. But he will want to satisfy himself
of the accuracy of the figures you give him.

Loan companies and department stores may be less careful. The store, charging 1½% a month in interest, is willing to see you pay back slowly, so long as you keep paying. The loan company may cynically decide that it won't worry about overloaded borrowers as long as they have good jobs. If worst comes to worst, their loans can be "consolidated" and stretched out in time, giving the loan company that much more in interest payments. But even loan companies tend to get into a sweat about anyone who has committed more than 25% of his post-tax income to repaying his debts.

Lenders get their information about people who are trying to borrow by calling "credit investigation bureaus," which exist in every city and maintain files on borrowers, how fast they pay their bills, how often they get into trouble, how much they make, and how often they change jobs. There may also be other data in the files—nasty things like matrimonial disputes and arrest records.

This is an enormous data-keeping operation, and with people moving about so often, it's hard for purely local investigators to keep their files useful. Retail Credit Co. and Credit Data Co., now a subsidiary of the conglomerate company TRW, have computerized many of these files nationwide, and can offer local bureaus or lenders information on newcomers in town. Local credit bureaus have also been putting information into computer memory cores, for quick retrieval as needed. Banks, department stores, loan companies—all will make a credit investigation on you before they make a loan.

What the computer once learns about you the computer never forgets. It therefore behooves you to see that credit-bureau computers have no incorrect derogatory information about you, no matter how old.

A law professor wrote not long ago that the real danger of the computer was that "society would lose its benign capacity to forget." In the credit business in the 1970s, nothing is ever forgotten, and not much is forgiven. If false information gets into a man's credit bureau file, it can damage his life wherever he goes. Since early 1971, when the federal Fair Credit Reporting Act went into effect, credit bureaus have been required to let you look at what they are sending out on you, and to give you a chance to challenge it.

Your credit and your son's activism

According to an article in *The Wall Street Journal* in December 1971, the new law may not be making as much difference as it should. The article cites the cases of a suburban New York car dealer, a Tulsa newspaper reporter and a Dallas systems analyst, all of whom had trouble finding out why they were being denied credit—or, in the case of the Dallas man, losing out on job opportunities. In all three cases, the trail led back to a credit bureau's files and to inaccurate and negative statements dealing with things like the father's work habits and the son's political activism in high school. And considerable effort was required to get the credit bureau to show the file.

Remember that now *under the law* you do have the right to see what credit bureaus are sending out about you, to challenge anything that seems inaccurate, and to make them add your challenge to the file they send out to their customers.

Despite these problems, most borrowers are probably better off because such computerized files exist: they can get their loans faster, and if they move (as

It is now law that a credit bureau must show his own file to anyone who requests it. The bureaus are still reluctant to do so, however. Some desk pounding is indicated.

one out of five Americans does, every year) they can rapidly establish credit in their new neighborhoods.

Another thing lenders want to know is why you want the money. If, like the French painter Paul Gauguin, you're planning to quit your job as a bank teller and go off to Tahiti to paint, nobody is likely to lend you money for that. On the other hand, every lender loves the borrower who wants the money for a "home improvement" loan, a new bedroom or a better kitchen or a swimming pool, which will increase his assets and tie him a little more tightly to his neighborhood.

One of the oldest reasons for borrowing is to invest the money at a return you hope will be greater than the interest you pay on the loan.

Stock market professionals normally buy "on margin," which means that they borrow part of the price of the stocks and bonds they buy. Here the amount of the loan you can make is controlled, obviously, by the market price of the securities—and also by the Federal Reserve System, which establishes a "margin requirement" (fluctuating in normal times between 40% and 75%). The margin requirement expresses the percentage of the price of his purchase the customer must put up himself; the rest (from 60% to 25%, according to the regulation at the time) he can borrow. New York Stock Exchange rules require interest rates on margin loans to be at least ½% above the prime rate—5% in early 1972. That rate is for the best customer; the average margin customer probably pays 1% above prime rate. The broker's profit comes not from the loan, but from the extra commission income received from bigger purchases.

Trying to change a computer's appraisal of your credit-worthiness can be frustrating. You have to get at the people behind the computer.

Paul Gauguin, the famous Frenchman who gave up a workaday job to move to Tahiti to paint, would have been considered a poor credit risk, though his paintings eventually sold for huge sums.

Experience, especially during the crash of 1929, has shown that this sort of borrowing for investment is very dangerous for the run-of-the-mine investor, but the brokers and their banks (who are protected by the security itself, pledged to the loan) are willing to lend the money.

It's illegal to borrow elsewhere any money you use to pay for your part of the price of a stock bought on a margin account.

CHAPTER IX

How Much *Should* You Borrow?

Probably the most important element in anyone's long-term happiness is how well he knows himself. Misunderstanding one's own talents and aptitudes is the most common cause of getting into the wrong line of work, probably even of making the wrong marriage.

Everybody daydreams a little, but people who make money decisions on the basis of their daydreams find the world a cold, hard place when they wake up. Nowhere is this more certain than in borrowing.

Sociologists who have looked at the credit system find that most people borrow sensibly. It's between the ages of 25 and 34, when they're having children, equipping households and moving ahead in the world, that people are most likely to borrow. Three-quarters of all families headed by a man in that age group are paying off installment loans. That's the age

Financial daydreams can be heartwarming but they make poor collateral for loans from institutions—which never have daydreams about anything.

when men are likely to be promoted to better-paying jobs, or simply to rise along the salary schedule by seniority. If you can count on having more money next year, you can more safely undertake to borrow money you will have to pay back next year. Of families headed by men or women over 65, only about one-fifth are paying off installment loans. Their income isn't going to rise, they may face serious medical expenses not covered by Medicare, and any debt they incur now is likely to be a burden to them next year.

Bankers, who have to play safe, look at the borrower's current income. Borrowers can look at their

To young families growing and moving up the
financial ladder, installment loans
are like members of the household.

expectations for next year's income—provided they have a temperament that allows them to look ahead honestly, considering not only the extra money they can count on receiving, but also any extra expense they must expect to incur. If the baby on the way is going to require moving to another house with bigger mortgage payments, it's worse than foolish—it's borrowing trouble as well as money—to take a vacation trip to Europe on credit, however attractive the airline makes the trip look in its brochures. On the other hand, if the youngest of the kids is about to start school and the mother of the household knows she can go back to that job at the electric light company which she left when she had the oldest girl, there's no serious reason not to anticipate the new income a little and see Venice in the springtime.

In general, if you have been saving money, you can figure that under the pressure to pay back a loan you'll probably be able to put aside about twice what you've been saving.

If you've never been able to save, you should have some very good idea of where you're going to find the money to make payments before you undertake a loan. And, of course, if you're now struggling to pay off what you owe you should avoid like a disease any temptation to undertake new debt.

The question of how much you have to rely on yourself in an emergency should also enter into these calculations. A New York City subway worker can count on his employer to pick up virtually all expenses in connection with any family illness—the union contract includes hospitalization, surgical and other health benefits. Moreover, even if he's getting on in years he can risk undertaking loan commitments, because the Transit Authority's retirement plan plus Social Security income will probably ensure that his income doesn't go down at all after he stops working.

What you do not need when the load of debt is
a crushing weight is another loan, no
matter how attractive the terms appear to be.

A lawyer or an accountant, however, may have nothing to fall back on but his own savings if illness strikes or retirement time comes.

The bankers' rules of thumb on what they want to lend are also reasonable guides to what a family ought to borrow. For a necessity like a car, it may be possible to stretch up to 15%: the fact that you are giving up other things for the practical value and fun of an automobile makes it easier to accept the givings-up. But if you've got to give up going to the movies tonight or buying a party dress because of a vacation you took last year, you're likely to resent the burden and to begin thinking about postponing payments.

The debt counselor

A rule of thumb that relates borrowing capacity to monthly payments means you can borrow more on longer-term loans. If you get into trouble one of the first things a debt-counselor will suggest is a program to stretch out your repayments. (Most social service agencies do have someone who is skilled in debt counseling. If you're in trouble on a bank loan, the bank itself will probably have someone who can go over your problem with you and suggest steps for you to take to ease the situation.)

But longer-term loans always mean more money paid for interest, both ways: there are more months in which interest must be paid, and the interest rate itself will probably be higher. Except for a house, any loan lasting more than two years can be dangerous. It may be better to buy a cheaper car or a used car and pay it off in two years than to get into 36-month auto loan programs.

The thing to avoid is endangering the fabric of your daily life. In most states, a lender can garnishee part of your wages (limited by federal law in 1971 to 25% of the take-home pay or the amount of take-home pay over $48, whichever is the lesser). This forces your employer to pay to your creditor as well as to you every time there is a paycheck. In the old days the nuisance this caused your employer often led him to fire you, but a new federal law forbids this. There is no doubt, however, that it puts a black mark next to your name in employment records.

If you come to the end of your string in debts, you *can* go bankrupt. There's a "Chapter XIII" kind of semi-bankruptcy in which a federal court acts as a debt counselor and stretches out your payments. The court makes you pay promptly each installment of the stretched loan under the threat of *real* bankruptcy the minute you miss a payment. Actual bankruptcy does excuse your debts, this once (you can't do it again for at least seven years), but only at the price of auctioning off most of your personal possessions that might have a resale value.

Bankruptcy is less than suicide, and bad luck makes

An employer must hand over part of an employee's
paycheck to a creditor (of the employee)
who obtains a court garnishment order. But the law
limits the amount that can be garnisheed.

bankrupts of many people whose lives are both com-
mercially and personally blameless. It's cruel and unfair to hold a bankruptcy against anyone, and most
people have learned not to be prejudiced against
those who have gone through this experience. But it
is a horrible experience.

One way a loan can damage the fabric of your daily
life is the small print on a "chattel mortgage" undertaken when you buy furniture, television sets, major
appliances and the like.

Some stores write into these loans a pledge of *all* your resalable household goods, not just a pledge of what you are buying now. That means that if you fail to make the payments on the living room furniture, they can "repossess" the television set, too, even though you don't owe a penny on it.

Especially in low-income neighborhoods, where many people are almost illiterate or don't speak English well, storekeepers have been known to prey on

A chattel mortgage can deprive you not only of goods you fail to pay for but also of possessions you *have* paid for.

their credit customers, selling them defective furniture and then, when they quite properly refuse to pay for damaged goods, cleaning them out of the few precious possessions they have. The spread of poverty program law offices has diminished the incidence of this sort of deception, and the Truth in Lending Act now makes all installment loan forms spell out in easy-to-read type exactly what is being pledged behind the loan.

> Under no circumstances should anyone buy on a time contract which specifically endangers his continued possession of the household goods he has already bought and paid for.

Different as they are from business loans, personal loans should be made on rather similar principles. The businessman borrows to make (or stock) what he expects to sell tomorrow, planning to pay back the loan out of the proceeds of the sale. The individual borrows to enjoy today what he expects to be able to pay for tomorrow. If the businessman doesn't feel confident that he can sell what he buys with the money he borrows, he shouldn't (and won't) undertake the loan. If the individual can't see clearly where in next year's expenses he will be able to fit the repayments of his loan, he shouldn't risk his future for what will turn out to have been brief and unsatisfactory pleasures.

The rules of thumb for the borrower, then, are: 1) the proportion of next year's next-to-certain income pledged to the repayment of loans (other than home mortgages) should rarely if ever exceed 15%, and should usually be kept under 10%; 2) the need for or desire for what is being bought should be great enough to justify the future sacrifices that may be necessary to pay for it; 3) the income expected for next year should be higher (*never lower*) than this year's income.

CHAPTER X

Free Credit

A great deal of the borrowing everybody does requires no interest payment at all, and isn't usually thought of as borrowing. Every time you make a long-distance phone call, you are in effect buying on credit from the telephone company, which will not be billing you for the call until another month or so has passed. Electricity, milk (in places where the milkman still exists), the services of most doctors and dentists, the home-delivered newspaper, and everything you buy at a store where you have an old-fashioned charge account—all these can be considered examples of interest-free borrowing. Except that there's

With a handful of Travel and Entertainment
cards, the living can be as easy as floating
in a balloon in a cloudless sky—at least
for a while.

still no Santa Claus. For most of these services, you do
pay in one way or another, because the costs of giving
you "free credit" are built into the prices you are
charged. Still, the telephone company and the power
company and the stores buy *their* credit wholesale, at
rates much lower than you yourself as an individual
would have to pay.

The first example of "free credit" that most people think of these days is the credit card, especially the "T & E"—travel and entertainment—cards issued by Diners Club, Carte Blanche, and American Express; the oil company credit cards; and the "bank cards" issued as Master Charge, Unicard, BankAmericard, and others. The principle here, very cleverly worked out by Diners Club, the earliest of these ventures, was that the suppliers—the restaurants and hotels and airlines and shops—would be willing to pay the cost of providing credit to their customers, because the customers would spend more if they didn't have to pay cash. The supplier sends the sales slip to the credit company, which immediately pays him for what you bought—less 5% or 7½%, depending on the credit company, the nature of the service involved, and maybe how badly the credit company wants this name to advertise as among those outfits that "honor" his card.

A slice for the credit company

Not all T & E cards, of course, are "free"—you pay $15 a year for the right to carry Diners, Carte Blanche, and American Express. And it's clear enough that the hotels and restaurants and stores that accept the cards put something extra on the prices to make up for the 5% or 7½% they must give the credit company. The price increase probably won't be as much as the discount to the credit company, because many of the sales are still made to cash customers, and the store has to charge the same list price to everyone.

It sometimes happens that a store which ac-
cepts a credit card will give you a discount of
3%, maybe even 5%, if you offer to pay cash
instead.

The bank cards are free; in fact, the banks spread
them around the country like confetti when they first
got into this business, thereby saddling themselves
with enormous losses from mail thieves and dead-
beats. But unlike the T & E companies, which are not
geared to charge you interest on late balances
(though they will dun you frantically for what you
owe if you pay late, and may even cancel the card),
the bank cards are set up to charge interest, at the
department store rate of 1½% per month, if you
don't pay up within 25 days after the billing date.
(This means, incidentally, that you can sometimes
have the use of their money for nearly two months
before you start paying interest, and if you pay in full
before the due date the "loan" is interest-free.)

Most bank cards have a limit of $500, unless special
arrangements are made. T & E cards, partly because
they are often used for big-ticket expenses like trans-
continental or transatlantic flying, don't announce
any maximum figure to cardholders. But the storekeepers and airlines have guidelines from the credit
company, and over a certain figure ($300 at a single
store, $500 for airplane tickets are the usual numbers)

the cardholder will find himself waiting a while for the clerk to return from the telephone to query the operators of the T & E card about whether purchases of this size should be permitted on your account. If you don't look prosperous, $100 may be enough to trigger a mini-investigation over the phone.

For anyone who can take tax deductions for any of the expenses paid for with a credit card, all the cards have great extra value as records that will completely

Establishments that honor credit cards sometimes will offer a discount to a cash customer. It's worth asking.

satisfy the man from the Internal Revenue Service. But it's important to write on the back of the credit sales slip the reason why this expense should be tax-deductible, so you can correlate your appointments diary and your deductions if a revenooer calls you in for an audit.

Another advantage of the T & E cards for travelers is that they permit the cashing of personal checks in far-off places, up to a limit of $500. To keep this privilege from being a pure nuisance, the T & E companies

For a big-ticket purchase on a credit card, a telephone call is in order to make sure your account can carry all that weight.

usually require that anything over $50 be taken in the form of travelers checks rather than in cash. That's no great hardship: you're probably better off carrying travelers checks anyway, and the 1% fee usually charged for the purchase of travelers checks is a small enough price to pay for the right to cash a personal check in a town where not a soul knows who you are and you don't even speak the language. Incidentally, you can sometimes get travelers checks free from a savings and loan where you have an account and from Barclay's Bank, a British bank seeking to break into the American market.

Another advantage of the T & E credit card became apparent in 1971, when the world monetary system went into a state of severe shock during the middle of the tourist season. Because the T & E company pays off in the currency of the country where the sale was made, T & E cards were accepted on days when U.S. currency or travelers checks in dollars were spurned.

The gasoline credit cards started off as a promotion device for the companies, which tried to get you to use their brand (of tires and accessories, as well as gas) in return for the offer of credit. By the 1970s, however, the oil companies had become more ambitious. Most of them have arrangements with motels and hotel chains to accept the card for accommodations (the motel and hotel chains then pay the oil companies 5% of your bill, as they would pay a T & E company), and many of them also have mail-order businesses on the side, offering merchandise to be charged against the credit card. (A number of airlines also have credit cards that are used this way.) The oil company cards are still domestic only, however; if you take a car abroad or rent one there, you'll have to pay cash for your gas. Since 1970, the oil and airline companies have programed their computers to charge interest—again, at 1½% per month on the unpaid balance—on any account outstanding more than 30 days.

Credit cards are particularly handy to have in out-of-the-way places where you are unknown and a foreigner as well.

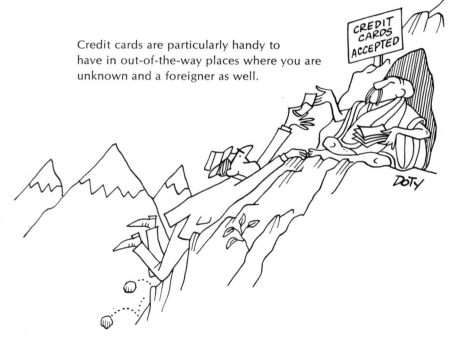

CHAPTER XI

Tricks of the Trade

It's not unreasonable that any company which offers you "free" credit (the technical name is an "open account") should begin charging interest if the bill remains unpaid after a certain length of time. In the future, as business machinery improves in capability, you can expect that all the bills you used to be able to delay a while without penalty will begin to carry an interest charge.

It is important to you to make sure they don't start the interest charge too soon.

The federal government had to move against the big mail-order houses to make them wait until 30 days had elapsed before beginning that monotonous and expensive run of 1½ % credit charges. Moreover, the bank cards operate differently in different states. In California, some of them are tied in to your bank account, and the moment the sales slip you signed is received at the bank your account is debited by that

It's a law: on revolving credit charge accounts interest cannot be levied before 30 days after the purchase has been made.

amount, which means that you don't get any credit at all, just a kind of check-guarantee service. Among the questions you want to ask before you accept the use of a bank credit card is how the bank expects to collect from you, and how much time you have to pay the bills before they begin to accumulate interest.

At department stores, too, watch out for the early whistle. In most states, if the store offers an "open account" for 30 days to charge customers, it can't start assessing interest on any item purchased until the 30 days are up. It's not easy arguing with a computer, but a letter to the president of the store may get results.

Borrowing money is like buying; and in all buying, there's no substitute for shopping around if you want to save money. Always start with the lowest-cost loan you can get—on your life insurance or savings or stock ownership—and don't use small loan companies unless you must. It's important to be sure that you buy what you want, rather than permitting yourself to be sold what somebody else wants you to buy.

There's one kind of very short loan that can actually save you money. Most savings banks pay interest on your savings only at the end of a calendar quarter, and any money withdrawn before that date (or before the start of a "grace period" that may begin three days earlier) will lose the interest it has earned.

If you plan to withdraw money from your savings account less than a month before the end of a quarter (that is, in March, June, September, or December), you'll come out ahead borrowing on your passbook for the rest of that month or up to the date of the grace period rather than taking the cash.

The three months interest you will receive on your account, which remains untouched until the date the loan comes due, will amount to more than the interest you pay the savings bank for the passbook loan.

Supermarkets don't have money racks but it pays you to shop for loans somewhat the way you shop for, say, frozen foods: compare the prices!

On the date when your account qualifies for the interest you have earned, the bank automatically credits your account with the interest, and deducts from your new, larger balance the amount of the passbook loan. For example, let's say you have a $1,000 savings account which pays 5%, compounded and credited quarterly. You need $1,000 for the last month of the quarter. The bank will lend you that at 7%. At the end of the quarter your savings account has earned $12.50. The interest for one month on your passbook loan will be $5.83. You've had the use of $1,000 for a month, your savings account is intact, and you've made $6.67 in interest.

Little things you hardly notice make an annoying difference. When you are borrowing cash, for example, some lenders just make a loan and others make a loan "at discount." Let's say both seem to be charging $60 for $1,000. The straight loan gives you $1,000 and asks you to pay back $1,060 in 12 monthly installments; the discount loan gives you $940 and asks you to pay back $1,000. The true interest rate on the first of these is just over 11%; on the second, it's just under 12%. And if you had figured out that you needed $1,000, the first of them gives you what you need, while the second does not.

Always sign up for the shortest term of loan and the maximum monthly payment you're sure you can make.

It's true you can conserve some current credit by taking longer loans, enabling you to keep buying even though you're still paying off on a previous purchase—but that's exactly the temptation you want to avoid. And getting the car or the TV paid for more quickly will put you back in the market sooner for the dishwasher or the camping equipment, if that's what you want next. The shorter the loan, the less the proportion of your total expenditure that must be wasted on interest.

Watch out for the loan with a "balloon" at the end—a last payment larger than the other payments, which may force you to borrow again for the same purpose.

Ballooning your way to the poorhouse

A balloon may make sense for a businessman, or in a short mortgage at high interest rates, when you think you'll want to refinance in a few years, anyway. But it's the road to the poorhouse in personal loans.

Watch out, too, for loading "current" costs onto a capital investment. If you want a service contract to go with your new washing machine, well and good: buy one. But don't allow the seller to add the costs of the contract onto your purchase loan—that just means you have to pay more for the service. The first three months you use the washing machine it will be covered by the manufacturer's warranty, anyway, and there's no reason to buy a service contract until the warranty is about to expire. In any event, there's not much point in buying a service contract unless you expect to renew it year after year—the odds are that a new appliance won't need service during its first year. If you're going to have to pay cash for the service contract in later years, it's wise to get into the habit of doing so from the beginning.

One of the most convincing reasons for borrowing is to take advantage of a sale on something you're going to buy anyway, but make sure it's a real sale.

The cost of a service contract added on to an installment purchase of an appliance is an add-on that should be firmly resisted.

Unless you drive a car more than four years before trading it in, the annual end-of-model-year extra reductions advertised as 10% in the auto showroom are no bargain at all.

When you come to trade in the car for a new one three years later, you'll find that it's treated like any other car of its model year, even if it was the last off the line. Four years after you bought the car, dealers evaluating it for trade-in will deduct from its list price a figure so much larger than the one they would deduct from the list price of the first car that came off the line in the next model year that your 10% savings actually turn into a loss.

Always ask for loans that can be paid off at any time for no more (or very little more) than the outstanding balance.

Except for the life insurance loan and the passbook loan (and maybe the margin loan on Wall Street), all of which can be paid off at any time without penalty, the interest you have to pay on a loan will always be higher than what you can expect to earn safely on your own money. If you get a windfall—if a rich uncle dies in California, or a cut in the federal income tax rates brings you a refund in April—you should be able to use the money to cancel out a high-interest debt.

Remember the long-term advantages of the old-fashioned mortgage that reduces your principal in equal installments, especially if you're getting on in years and you feel you can pay more now than you'll be able to pay later. Make sure you can refinance a high-interest mortgage, which means, in practice, that you want the right to pay off the principal in full, without penalty, at any time after, say, the first two or three years.

An old mortgage at a low rate is something to be cherished. It makes the house attractive to buyers when you need to sell.

And if you're borrowing on a mortgage in a low-interest period, try to get advance agreement from the bank that the transfer of the mortgage to anyone who buys your house "will not unreasonably be refused."

Then, if interest rates go up, your house is worth more to prospective purchasers—that is, they can afford to pay you more because the carrying charges are lower. Banks don't want to make such promises, which they call "assumption and release agreements," because they'd rather be free to make a new mortgage with your customer at a higher rate. For them, it's a one-way ratchet—they're stuck with the low-interest loan if rates go up. Still, it's worth a try. In the absence of such a clause, you can risk keeping your name on the mortgage bond and continuing to owe the money to the bank if the buyer later defaults. This is probably safe in most cases (though scary); just make sure you have the right to cancel out and make the buyer refinance for himself if he ever misses a mortgage payment or fails to maintain adequate homeowner's insurance.

Conversely, if you're buying an older house with a low-interest mortgage, try to persuade the owner to let the mortgage stand.

It may be worth taking a short second mortgage to pay part of the purchase price (even though second mortgage interest rates are very high) to retain the low monthly payments of the mortgages written before the mid-1960s.

Moving to a new town, it may well make sense to take a small loan soon after your arrival, from the bank that holds your mortgage and knows you or from a department store on a revolving credit plan, and pay it back fast, to establish a local credit rating.

For a newcomer to a community it makes sense to take out a loan, even if it is not needed. Paying it back quickly establishes a credit rating.

Some of the worst problems people have when they want to borrow money come not from some bad episode in their past, but from no record of their past that anybody in their present location can find. As the computerized services improve, this sort of foundation-digging to establish credit should become unnecessary in the future. But we haven't yet reached that promised land.

CHAPTER XII

The Art of Thinking about Money

Above all, watch your own attitude toward money. Too many people fall into one of two groups—either they take money too seriously, and allow money worries to poison their lives, or they borrow too freely because what they want to do seems so much more urgent to them than the question of how they are going to pay for it. Often enough, people who start off in this second group wind up in the first. Both are wrong.

Money is both a measurement and a commodity, and the psychological difference between its two

functions confuses many people. Seeking money because of some notion that making more means being
"better" is a classic path to unhappiness: people
whose only satisfaction in their work is the paycheck
lead miserable lives. Even when a job isn't interesting
in itself, most working people find satisfaction in the

When you have a growing family that might call
for a bigger house—and a bigger mortgage—
should you fly now on credit?

social life that surrounds almost any modern job, the relations with the others in the office or the shop; and it's not at all uncommon for people to prefer a congenial working atmosphere to a few dollars more in the envelope. The man who drives himself to grab overtime, or takes a second job at the price of physical exhaustion and a hurried home life, is often using money as a measurement, a way to bolster his self-esteem, and he pays too high a price for it. But working to buy something you know you want—whether you're a kid with a paper route paying off a bicycle or a housewife wrapping parcels part-time in a department store to pay for a trip to Europe—carries a reward beyond the dollars-and-cents themselves.

Knowing your objective is important in everything you do, and money isn't a sensible objective in itself; even as a commodity, it's just a means to an end.

Credit and savings are closely related: put into a single sentence, the work of the Federal Reserve System is to keep a balance between the total savings and the total borrowings in the country. But they're also closely related in any individual's life. Though there are emergencies in which credit dries up just when you need it—the loss of a job or the illness of a breadwinner—for most purposes it's worth about as much to be a good credit risk as it is to have savings.

Day in, day out, your borrowing power is as much a financial asset as the money you have in the bank. Either can be used to buy what you want when you want it.

Just as you wouldn't squander your savings without thinking about whether this fur coat or sports car or round-the-world cruise is really what you want to do with the money you struggled to put aside, you shouldn't use up your borrowing power on impulse. Consumer credit and self-amortizing mortgages are American inventions, and they are not the least of the reasons why the average American lives better than the average citizen of any other country on earth. The value of money is what it buys. In the end, using credit wisely is like using cash wisely—you have to be sure that what you buy is worth what you pay for it. Paying a little more to enjoy now what you could not otherwise enjoy until later can be a monetary decision as wise as any other, or as foolish. The more intelligently you make that decision, the more cheerfully you can greet each new and interesting day.

CHAPTER XIII

Read the Print—Fine and Otherwise!

The subject covered in this volume is unavoidably associated with myriad forms: applications, legal notifications, interest tabulations, mortgage-payment tables, credit analyses, and so on *ad infinitum* and, as far as the average citizen is concerned, *ad nauseam* as well.

This is unfortunate for the average citizen, for the fine print he often does not read is vital to his financial well-being. The editors have therefore selected for this chapter some important credit forms and tabulations, etc., for you to examine at leisure — instead of hastily scanning them when thrust at you to be signed.

Q. and A. re Z

The borrower's best friend is Regulation Z, otherwise known as the federal Truth in Lending Act or Consumer Credit Cost Disclosure. But because the borrower may be unaware of this friend's existence, there are printed on the following pages sections from

What you ought to know about

FEDERAL RESERVE REGULATION

Z

This is a pamphlet prepared by no less an august source than the Governors of the Federal Reserve System for the *use of creditors* so that they may know what the law requires of them. From this *you the consumer-borrower* may learn what you are entitled to. (For complete copies of the pamphlet write or call the nearest office of the Federal Trade Commission.) Some of the italics have been supplied by the editors.

About this pamphlet

If you extend consumer credit, then you must become familiar with Regulation Z on Truth in Lending. You will be responsible, as a creditor, for complying with the regulation.

Its purpose

The purpose of Regulation Z is to let borrowers and customers know the cost of your credit so that they can compare your costs with those of other credit sources and avoid the uninformed use of credit. Regulation Z does not fix maximum, minimum, or any charges for credit.

Two important points to bear in mind

The finance charge and the annual percentage rate are really the two most important disclosures required by this regulation. They tell your customer, at a glance, how much he is paying for his credit and its relative cost in percentage terms.

The businesses affected

Regulation Z applies to: banks, savings and loan associations, department stores, credit card issuers, credit unions, automobile dealers, consumer finance companies, residential mortgage brokers, and *craftsmen—such as plumbers and electricians. It also applies to doctors, dentists and other professional people,* and hospitals. In fact to any individual or organization that extends or arranges credit for which a finance charge is or may be payable or which is repayable in more than four installments.

Enforcement

Specific responsibilities for enforcement of Regulation Z are divided among nine federal agencies. A complete list of these agencies and the types of businesses they cover follows this section.

Penalties under the Truth in Lending Act

If you fail to make disclosures as required under this legislation, *your customer may sue you for twice the amount of the finance charge*—for a minimum of $100, up to a maximum of $1,000—plus court costs and attorney's fees. And if you willfully or knowingly disobey the law or Regulation Z and are convicted you could be fined up to $5,000, or be imprisoned for one year, or both.

Some general questions and answers

Q: What types of credit are covered under Regulation Z?

A: Generally, credit you extend to people for personal, family, household or agricultural uses, not exceeding $25,000. But ALL real estate credit transactions for these purposes are covered regardless of the amount.

Q: What types of credit are not covered?

A: The following are not affected by Regulation Z:
   1. Business and commercial credit—except agricultural credit.
   2. Credit to federal, state and local governments. (However, governmental units extending credit to individuals are affected by this law.)
   3. Transactions in securities and commodities accounts with a broker dealer registered with the Securities & Exchange Commission.
   4. Transactions under certain public utility tariffs.
   5. Credit over $25,000—except real estate transactions.

Q: Can a state law be substituted for Regulation Z?

A: Yes it can, provided the Federal Reserve Board makes that determination as provided by law. Any determination made will be published.

Q: What happens if I not only follow Regulation Z but also elect to follow inconsistent state law?

A: In these cases the state disclosure may be shown on a separate sheet. They may also be shown on the same statement as the federal disclosures. But in this event they must appear separately and below the federal disclosure, *clearly marked that they are inconsistent* with the federal disclosures, and separated by a dividing line.

Q: What terms are used to describe credit transactions in the regulation?

A: The regulation divides all consumer credit transactions into two broad categories; open end credit, and credit other than open end. These are discussed in subsequent sections of these Questions and Answers.

Q: How long do I have to keep records?

A: You should keep evidence of compliance for two years.

Q: Will anyone inspect my records?

A: If asked by the proper agency you must show your records relating to disclosure and evidence of compliance.

Some questions and answers on the finance charge and annual percentage rate

Q: What is the finance charge?

A: It is the total of all costs which your customer must pay, directly or indirectly, for obtaining credit.

Q: What costs are included in the finance charge?

A: Here are some of the more common items that you must include in your finance charge.

1. Interest
2. Loan fee.
3. Finder's fee or similar charge.
4. Time price differential.
5. Amount paid as a discount.
6. Service, transaction or carrying charge.
7. Points.
8. Appraisal fee (except in real estate transactions).
9. Premium for credit life or other insurance, should you make this a condition for giving credit.
10. Investigation or credit report fee (except in real estate transactions).

Q: Are all costs part of the finance charge?

A: No, some costs which would be paid if credit were not employed may be excluded. However, you must itemize and show them to your customer. Here are a few examples:

1. Taxes.
2. License fees.
3. Registration fees.
4. Certain title fees and other legal fees.
5. Some real estate closing fees.

Q: In what form is the finance charge to be shown to the customer?

A: It must be clearly typed or written, stating the dollars and cents total and the annual percentage rate. *The words "finance charge" and "annual percentage rate" must stand out* especially clear. In the sale of dwellings, the total dollar finance charge need not be stated, although the annual percentage rate must be included.

Q: What is the annual percentage rate?

A: Simply put, it is the relative cost of credit in percentage terms.

Q: Are maximum or minimum rates specified in Regulation Z?

A: No. *Regulation Z does not fix maximum, minimum,* or any charges for credit. But it requires that you show whatever rate you do charge.

Q: How accurate must the annual percentage rate be?

A: Accurate to the *nearest one quarter of one percent.*

Q: How is the annual percentage rate computed?

A: It depends on whether the credit is open end or other than open end credit.

Some questions and answers about open end credit

Q: What is open end credit?

A: Typically it covers most credit cards and revolving charge accounts in retail stores, where finance charges are usually made on unpaid amounts each month.

Q: What must an open end credit customer be told under this law?

A: If it is a *new* account, then your customer must receive these specific items in writing to the extent applicable:
1. The conditions under which the finance charge may be imposed and the period in which payment can be made without incurring a finance charge.
2. The method used in determining the balance on which the finance charge is to be made.
3. How the actual finance charge is calculated.

    4. The periodic rates used and the range of balances
to which each applies.

    5. The conditions under which additional charges may
be made along with details of how they are
calculated.

    6. *Descriptions of any lien which you may acquire on a
customer's property.*

    7. The minimum payment that must be made on
each billing.

Q: What about customers who already have open end accounts on July 1, 1969?

A: The same information must be sent to them by July 31 if the account has an unpaid balance on July 1. Where no balance is owed on that date, the same information must be supplied on or before the first billing that follows use of the account.

Q: Are periodic statements necessary on open end accounts?

A: Yes, but only where there is an unpaid balance over $1 or where a finance charge is made.

Q: What sort of information must accompany a monthly statement?

A: Where applicable, you must give customers this information:

    1. The unpaid balance at the start of the billing period.

    2. The amount and date of each extension of credit
and identification of each item bought.

    3. Payments made by a customer and other credits; this
includes returns, rebates and adjustments.

    4. *The finance charge shown in dollars and cents.*

    5. The rates used in calculating the finance charge plus
the range of balances to which they apply.

    6. The *annual percentage rate.*

    7. The *unpaid balance* on which the finance charge
was calculated.

8. The *closing date of the billing cycle* and the unpaid balance at that time.

Q: Where must this information appear?

A: Some items must appear on the actual face of the statement. Others may be shown on the reverse side; or, on a separate form enclosed in the same envelope.

Q: How is the annual percentage rate determined on open end credit?

A: The finance charge is divided by the unpaid balance to which it applies. This gives the rate per month or whatever time period is used. The result is multiplied by 12 or the other number of time periods used by you during the year.

Here's an example:

A typical charge of 1½% is made on an unpaid balance where bills are sent out monthly. The annual percentage rate would be twelve times 1½% or 18%.

Some questions and answers about credit other than open end

Q: What types of credit are included?

A: Both loans and sales credit—in every case for a specified period of time where the total amount, number of payments, and due dates are agreed upon by you and your customer. Typically, it is used in buying or financing the purchase of *"big ticket" items.* A good example is a loan from a finance company to buy *an automobile.* Another example is credit extended by a store to buy a *washing machine, a television set,* or other major appliance. It also includes a *single payment loan.*

Q: What must the credit customer be told in these types of transactions?

A: You must present to your customer in writing the following information as applicable, plus additional information relating to the type of credit extended.

1. The total dollar amount of the finance charge; except in the case of a credit transaction to finance purchase of a dwelling.
2. The date on which the finance charge begins to apply, if this is different from the date of the transaction.
3. The annual percentage rate.
4. The number, amounts and due dates of payments.
5. The total payments—except in the case of first mortgages on dwelling purchases.
6. The amount you *charge for any default,* delinquency, etc. or method you use for calculating that amount.
7. Description of *any security you will hold.*
8. Description of any *penalty charge for prepayment* of principal.
9. How the unearned part of the finance charge is calculated in the case of prepayment. Charges deducted from any rebate or refund must be stated.

Q: Are there any other things customers must be told?

A: That depends on the transaction—whether it is a loan or a credit sale.

Q: In the case of a loan, what do I have to tell my customers?

A: In addition to the information given your customer, as previously indicated, you must also provide this information:

1. The amount of credit to be given to your customer. This includes all charges which are part of the amount of credit extended but are not a part of the finance

charge. This information must be itemized.
2. Amounts that are deducted as prepaid finance charges and required deposit balances.

Q: Regarding credit sales, what additional information do I give these customers?

A: Again, you must give your customers all the information in the answer to the second question in this section, and the following additional information as applicable:
1. The cash price.
2. The down payment, including trade-in.
3. The difference between the two.
4. All other charges, itemized, that are included in the amount financed but not part of the finance charge.
5. The unpaid balance.
6. Amounts deducted as prepaid finance charges or required deposit balances.
7. The amount financed.
8. The total cash price, finance and all other charges. (This does not apply to the sale of a dwelling.)

Q: When must customers receive all this information on loan or credit sales?

A: Before the credit is extended.

Q: Must this information be given to customers in writing?

A: Yes. You must include the *information on the face of the note* or other instrument evidencing the obligation, or on a separate sheet that identifies the transaction.

Q: Are monthly statements required?

A: No. But if you do send out monthly statements, you must show clearly the annual percentage rate, and the period in which a payment must be made to avoid late charges.

Q: How is the annual percentage rate calculated on loans or credit other than open end?

A: By the actuarial method—payments are applied first to interest due and any remainder is then applied to reduce principal.

Q: What are examples of the actuarial method?

A: Here are two simple examples:

1. A bank loan of $100 repayable in equal monthly installments over one year is made, at a 6% add-on finance charge. The annual percentage rate would be 11%. The borrower would repay $106 over one year. He would only have use of the full $100 until he made his first payment, and less and less each month as payments are made. The effect is that the actual annual percentage rate is almost twice the add-on percentage rate.

2. Using the same example as above with the 6% finance charge discounted in advance. The annual percentage rate would be 11½% because the customer would only receive $94 and have to repay $100. He would have full use of only $94 of the loan up to the time he makes his first payment.

Q: But isn't the actuarial method very complicated?

A: Yes, it is. Recognizing this, the Federal Reserve Board has prepared tables showing the annual percentage rate based on the finance charge and the number of weekly or monthly payments to be made. These tables are available from the Federal Reserve Board and Federal Reserve Banks at a nominal cost.

Q: Must I use the Board's Annual Percentage Rate tables?

A: No. You may wish to purchase specially prepared tables for your type of business from one of several table or chart publishers. Trade associations and financial institutions can be helpful also.

Q: Must the creditor always show the annual percentage rate?

A: Generally yes, except that on credit other than open end credit, if the finance charge is $5 or less, and applies to credit of $75 or less, it need not be shown. The same exception applies to a finance charge of $7.50 or less on credit of more than $75.

Some questions and answers about real estate

Q: Is real estate covered under Regulation Z?

A: Yes. All real estate credit *in any amount* is covered under this regulation when it is to an individual and not for business purposes, unless the business purpose is agriculture.

Q: Does real estate credit cover more than mortgages?

A: Yes, very definitely. Any credit transaction that involves any type of security interest in real estate of a consumer is covered.

Q: Are there any special provisions that apply to real estate credit?

A: Two basic points:
   1. You do not have to show the total dollar amount of the finance charge on a credit sale or first mortgage loan to finance the purchase of the customer's dwelling.
   2. In many instances, your customer has the right to cancel a credit arrangement within three business days if his residence is used as collateral for credit.

Q: Must a creditor inform his customer of the right to cancel?

A: Yes. He must furnish the Notice prescribed by the regulation.

Q: What must the customer do to cancel a transaction under the regulation?

A: A customer may cancel a transaction

    1. by signing and dating the Notice to customer required by Federal law, which he receives from the creditor, *and* either

        (a) mailing the Notice to the creditor at the address shown on the Notice,

or   (b) delivering the Notice to the creditor at the address shown on the Notice either personally or by messenger (or by other agents),

or   2. by sending a telegram to the creditor at the address shown on the Notice. A brief description of the transaction which the customer wishes to cancel should be included in the telegram.

or   3. by preparing a letter (or other writing) which includes a brief description of the transaction which he wishes to cancel, *and* either

        (a) mailing the letter (or other writing) to the creditor at the address shown on the Notice.

or   (b) delivering the letter (or other writing) to the creditor at the address shown on the Notice either personally or by messenger (or by other agents).

Q: What if the customer telephones that he is going to cancel?

A: *A telephone call to the creditor may not be used to cancel a transaction; WRITTEN notice of cancellation is required.* If the customer takes one of the above steps to cancel within the three day period, he has effectively cancelled the transaction.

Q: What if I haven't received the notice of cancellation in three days?

A: You should allow time for a mailed letter or telegram sent within the three day period to be delivered, and *determine that your customer has not cancelled the transaction.*

Q: Does this right of cancellation apply to a first mortgage on a residence?

A: A first mortgage to finance the purchase of your customer's residence carries *no right to cancel. However,* a first mortgage for any other purpose and a second mortgage on the same residence may be cancelled.

Q: What happens regarding cancellation in the case of a mechanic's lien or similar security interest acquired by a craftsman who works on credit?

A: Take a craftsman, for example, who charges his customers a finance charge or allows payment in more than four installments. His customer does have a right to cancel, but only within three business days. Unless there is an emergency *the craftsman should wait three days* before starting work.

Q: Suppose a customer needs emergency repairs and cannot wait for three days?

A: A customer may waive his right to cancel a credit agreement if credit is needed to meet a *bonafide personal financial emergency* and if failure to start repairs would endanger him, his family, or his property.

Federal Agencies

From the list that follows, you will be able to tell which federal agency covers your particular business. Any questions you have should be directed to that agency. These agencies are also responsible for enforcing Regulation Z.

National Banks

Comptroller of the Currency
United States Treasury Department
Washington, D.C. 20220

State Member Banks

Federal Reserve Bank serving the area in which the State member bank is located.

Nonmember Insured Banks

Federal Deposit Insurance Corporation Supervising Examiner for the District in which the nonmember insured bank is located.

Savings Institutions Insured by the FSLIC and Members of the FHLB System (except for Savings Banks insured by FDIC)

The FHLB's Supervisory Agent in the Federal Home Loan Bank District in which the institution is located.

Federal Credit Unions

Regional Office of the Bureau of Federal Credit Unions, serving the area in which the Federal Credit Union is located.

Creditors Subject to Civil Aeronautics Board

Director, Bureau of Enforcement
Civil Aeronautics Board
1825 Connecticut Avenue, N.W.
Washington, D.C. 20428

Creditors Subject to Interstate Commerce Commission

Office of Proceedings
Interstate Commerce Commission
Washington, D.C. 20523

Creditors Subject to Packers and Stockyards Act

Nearest Packers and Stockyards Administration area supervisor.

Retail, Department Stores, Consumer Finance Companies, and All Other Creditors

Truth in Lending
Federal Trade Commission
Washington, D.C. 20580

This is how it all can end for those who have borrowed not wisely but too well, as Othello might have put it.

→

RETHINKING A TRANSACTION

In any financial and/or credit transaction involving your home —a home improvement loan, a major repair such as a new roof, the construction of a swimming pool—the federal Truth in Lending law protects you from any hasty agreement you may have made. Let's suppose a contractor came to your home to give you an estimate on a re-roofing job. He did some measuring, did some calculations on the back of an envelope, muttered a few sentences to himself, then said it would cost $X. You said OK, he pulled out a form from his pocket, filled some things in and asked you to sign. You signed. That night, when your spouse arrived, you told him/her about this and the $X. Spouse: "My God! That's twice what it should be!" Fear not. The muttering contractor must by law give you a chance to cancel.

The form reproduced here in part carries the tongue-twisting label of "right of rescission"; the builder or contractor or bank is required to send it to you and thus provide you with an opportunity to back out of the deal, for any reason you want to, without any penalty.

NOTICE OF OPPORTUNITY TO RESCIND

Credit transaction evidenced by_____ dated _____
(NOTE OR LIEN CONTRACT & DEED OF TRUST OR RETAIL INSTALLMENT CONTRACT)

for $_____ for_____ months.

_____   _____
(CUSTOMER'S NAME)   (STREET ADDRESS, CITY & STATE, ZIP CODE)

Notice To Customer Required By Federal Law:

You have entered into a transaction on _____
(DATE)
which may result in a lien, mortgage, or other security interest on your home. You have a legal right under federal law to cancel this transaction, if you desire to do so, without any penalty or obligation within three business days from the above date or any later date on which all material disclosures required under the Truth in Lending Act have been given to you. If you so cancel the transaction, any lien, mortgage, or other security interest on your home arising from this transaction is automatically void. You are also entitled to receive a refund of any downpayment or other consideration if you cancel. If you decide to cancel this transaction, you may do so by notifying

_____
(NAME OF CREDITOR)

at_____
(ADDRESS OF CREDITOR'S PLACE OF BUSINESS)

by mail or telegram sent not later than midnight of _____.
(DATE)
You may also use any other form of written notice identifying the transaction if it is delivered to the above address not later than that time. This notice may be used for that purpose by dating and signing below.

I hereby cancel this transaction.

_____   _____
(DATE)   (CUSTOMER'S SIGNATURE)

EFFECT OF RESCISSION. When a customer exercises his right to rescind under paragraph (a) of this section*, he is not liable for any finance or other charge, and any security interest becomes void upon such a rescission. Within 10 days after receipt of a notice of rescission, the creditor shall return to the customer any money or property given as earnest money, downpayment, or otherwise, and shall take any action necessary or appropriate to reflect the termination of any security interest created under the transaction. If the creditor has delivered any property to the customer, the customer may retain possession of it. Upon the performance of the creditor's obligations under this section, the customer shall tender the property to the creditor, except that if return of the property in kind would be impracticable or inequitable, the customer shall tender its reasonable value. Tender shall be made at the location of the property or at the residence of the customer, at the option of the customer. If the creditor does not take possession of the property within 10 days after tender by the customer, ownership of the property vests in the customer without obligation on his part to pay for it.

(*Reference is to Section 226.9(a) of Federal Reserve Board Regulation Z, which provides for the right of rescission referred to in the above notice.)

APPLYING FOR A PERSONAL UNSECURED LOAN

Banks will make unsecured loans but first they want to know a good many details about your financial standing and/or the financial muddle you've got yourself into. On this and the following pages a typical application blank is reproduced.

PERSONAL LOAN APPLICATION

TO:

The information given by me (us) below is true and complete and   Approved_____
                                                                                    Date Credit
is given to induce you to grant credit of $_____for_____months   Information Requested_____

for the purpose of _____

_____

_____

Full Name (Print)_____Age_____ ☐ Married
                                                  ☐ Single   Spouse's   Number of
                                                  ☐ Div. or Widow Name_____ Dependents___

Present Address_____City_____Years_____Home Phone_____

If at above address less than
2 years, give former address _____City & State_____Years_____

Your   Monthly   Currently
Occupation_____Take Home Pay $_____Employed By_____Years_____Months_____

Business   Business
Address_____City & State_____Phone_____

Previously   Previous
Employed by_____Occupation_____Business Address_____Years_____Months_____

                              Driver's   Employee or
Social Security No._____License No._____Badge Number_____

Spouse's   Monthly   Business
Occupation_____Take Home Pay $_____Employed By_____Years_____Months_____Phone_____

                              ☐ Checking
Name of   ☐ Savings
Your Bank_____Branch_____ ☐ Loan   Other Income $_____Source_____

Automobile
Make(s)_____Year_____Model_____License No._____

Nearest Relative   Complete
Not Living With Me_____Relationship_____Address_____

CREDIT REFERENCES (Banks, Stores, Credit Unions, Finance Companies, etc.).
Include all debts now owing. Attach additional sheet if necessary.

FIRM NAME	ADDRESS OR BRANCH	ACCOUNT NO.	ORIGINAL AMOUNT	PRESENT BALANCE	MONTHLY PAYMENT
☐ HOME LOAN ☐ RENT					
2ND HOME LOAN					
AUTO LOAN					
OTHERS					

I authorize you to obtain any information you may require regarding the statements made in this application and agree that the application shall remain your property, whether the loan is granted or not. I hereby certify that all statements in this application are true and complete and are made for the purpose of obtaining credit. I agree to notify you of any material change in the statement as set forth, and this statement shall be construed by you to be a continuing statement of the condition of the undersigned until written notice to the contrary is received by you. It is further agreed that, at your option, all of the obligations of the undersigned owed to you, whether maker or co-maker, shall immediately become due and payable without demand or notice should the undersigned become insolvent, bankrupt, or should any of his property held by you be attached by legal proceedings.

I prefer to make payments on the_____day of each month.

DATE _____ SIGNATURE _____

FINANCIAL STATEMENT OF APPLICANT AS OF _____ 19 _____

I (we) own the following:		I (we) owe the following:	
Cash and Bank Accounts	$	Household Bills	$
Stocks and Bonds (Listed Below)	$	Installment Notes and Contracts	$
Real Estate (Listed Below)	$	Real Estate Loans	$
Autos	$	For Income Taxes	$
Other	$	Other	$
	$		$
Total Assets	$	Total Liabilities	$

My (our) Net Worth is $

_____

_____

_____

_____

FOR BANK USE ONLY

Balance payable in_____		Rate	
monthly payments of $_____		Borrower Requires	$
Beginning_____ 19_____		Credit Life Insurance Premium	$
and ending_____ 19_____			$
			$
Percentage of Fixed Charges to Income of Family Head_____%		TOTAL	$
To Combined Income_____%		Discount	$
		Loan Amount	$

COMMENTS OF APPROVING OFFICER:

_____

_____

_____

_____

_____

REGULATION "U"

Regulation "U" of the Federal Reserve System spells out the rules governing the extension of credit by banks on collateral loans. Borrowers depositing common stocks or convertible bonds as security must complete and sign Federal Reserve Form U-1, which is shown on the following pages. The bank and the Fed are particularly interested in the "purpose of the loan" as described in Form U-1. If the borrower's aim is to deposit stocks for a loan to buy additional stocks, Regulation "U" Section 221.4—Supplement explicitly limits the loan value of the pledged securities to a maximum of 20%.

Most other stock-secured loans, however, carry loan values from 25% up to 75%, depending on the rating of the collateral. One large bank lends 75% of a stock's total value provided the stock is listed on the New York or American Stock Exchanges and carries a Standard & Poor's ranking of A+, A, or A—. If the ranking is only B, B—, C+ or C, this bank drops the loan value to 25%.

Some banks will lend 75% of a B+ stock, but only 50% if the stock paid no dividend in the prior year. Mutual funds normally bring 25% to 75% depending on quality. U.S. Government bonds rated AAA and AA carry a 90% loan value with most banks.

Obscure stocks, especially those traded not on an exchange but over the counter, generally do not rate at all well as collateral for loans. But this is not true for all over-the-counter securities. The best course is to ascertain before you set out to borrow just what rating your securities have. Your broker should know.

Note: banks cannot lend against their own stock.

BOARD OF GOVERNORS OF THE FEDERAL RESERVE SYSTEM

STATEMENT OF PURPOSE OF A STOCK-SECURED
EXTENTION OF CREDIT BY A BANK
(FEDERAL RESERVE FORM U-1)

**A FALSE OR DISHONEST STATEMENT BY THE CUSTOMER OR THE
OFFICER OF THE BANK ON THIS FORM MAY BE PUNISHABLE BY
FINE OR IMPRISONMENT (U.S. CODE, TITLE 15, SECTION 78ff AND
TITLE 18, SECTION 1001)**

Instructions:

    (1) Please print or type (if space is inadequate attach separate sheet).

    (2) The term "stock" is defined in § 221.3 (*l*) of Regulation U.

    (3) Part I (3) and (4) need be filled in only if the purpose of the credit described in
Part I (1) is other than to purchase or carry margin stock.

    (4) In Part II "source of valuation" need be filled in only if such source is other than
regularly published information in journal of general circulation.

    (5) Part II need not be completed in the case of a credit of $5,000 or less which is not
for the purpose of purchasing or carrying margin stock. However, in such cases, Part I
must be completed as if Part II were completed.

Part I (to be completed by customer(s))

    (1) The purpose of this credit in the amount of $_____, secured in whole
or in part by the stock listed in Part II (A) and (B) is (describe in detail)_____

_____

_____

_____

    (2) This bank,_____, has outstanding, or has agreed to extend,
to the undersigned, the following credits in addition to the credit described on this form
(itemize and describe briefly, including amounts and collateral if any). If none, so state.

_____

    (3) Is any of the collateral listed in Part II (A) or (B) to be delivered, or has any such
collateral been delivered, from a bank, broker, dealer, or person other than the undersigned?

                                               Yes ☐ No ☐

If yes, from whom?_____Against payment?   Yes ☐ No ☐

    (4) Has any of the collateral listed in Part II (A) or (B) been owned less than six
months? Yes ☐   No ☐   If yes, identify all such collateral so owned._____

_____

**The undersigned has (have) read this form and hereby certifies and affirms that to the best
of my (our) knowledge and belief the information contained on this form is true, accurate,
and complete.**

SIGNED_____   SIGNED_____

    (Manual signature)   (Date)   (Manual signature)   (Date)

          (Print or type name)   (Print or type name)

Part II (to be completed by bank)

(A) Collateral consisting of stock, other than debt securities convertible into margin stock. The loan value of such stock under the current Supplement to Regulation U is_____ per cent.

No. of shares	Itemize separately by issue	Market price per share	Source of valuation	Total market price per issue

(B) Collateral consisting of debt securities convertible into margin stock. The loan value of such securities under the current Supplement to Regulation U is_____ per cent.

Par value	Itemize separately by issue	Market price	Source of valuation	Total market price per issue

(C) Other collateral.

Describe briefly (itemize where 10 per cent or more)	Current market value	Source of valuation	Good faith loan value

The undersigned, a duly authorized officer of the bank, is aware that this stock-secured credit may be subject to Regulation U, has read this form, has accepted the customer's statement on Part I in good faith as defined below*, and hereby certifies and affirms that to the best of his knowledge and belief all the information contained on this form is true, accurate, and complete.

Date_____   SIGNED_____
                                        (Manual signature)

_____
(Print or type name and title)

*Regulation U requires that the customer's statement on this form be accepted by an officer of the bank acting in good faith. Good faith requires that such officer (1) must be alert to the circumstances surrounding the credit, and (2) if he has any information which would cause a prudent man not to accept the statement without inquiry, has investigated and is satisfied that the statement is truthful. Among the facts which would require such investigation are receipt of the statement through the mail or from a third party.

THIS FORM MUST BE RETAINED BY THE BANK FOR AT LEAST THREE YEARS AFTER THE TERMINATION OF THIS CREDIT

PLEDGING SECURITIES AS COLLATERAL

The value of securities as collateral for loans varies from company to company. In evaluating stocks and bonds as collateral, most banks follow the rating of the company by Standard and Poor's, the well known financial reporting firm. The S and P rating is one factor in the bank's decision to lend and how much to lend. Another factor is where the stock is listed. Here are the Standard and Poor's ratings for various categories of securities. The ratings are expressed in letters and categories; the percentages indicate general loan values of the securities. Your broker or banker can give you the ratings of stocks you hold.

Ratings of Securities

Common Stocks

A+	Highest	75%
A	High	75%
A−	Above Average	75%
B+	Average	50%
B	Below Average	25%
B−	Low	25%
C	Lowest	25%
NR	No Ranking	

Preferred Stocks

AAA	Prime	75%
AA	High Grade	75%
A	Sound	75%
BBB	Medium Grade	50%
BB	Lower Grade	25%
B	Speculative	25%
C	Sub-Marginal	

Corporation Bonds

AAA	Highest Grade	85%
AA	High Grade	85%
A	Upper Medium Grade	80%
BBB	Medium Grade	80%
BB	Lower Medium Grade	50%
B	Speculative	25%

CCC-CC	Outright Speculations
C	Income Bonds Paying No Interest
DDD-D	Bonds in Default

Mutual Funds

Quality Common Stock Funds	High Loan Value	75%
Balanced Funds	High Loan Value	75%
Bond & Preferred Stock Funds	High Loan Value	75%
Performance Funds	Moderate Loan Value	50%
Specialized Funds	Moderate Loan Value	50%
Hedge Funds	Low Loan Value	25%

DO-IT-YOURSELF CREDIT RATING

Banks, credit reporting bureaus and other financial institutions sometimes use "point" systems to rate the credit-worthiness of individuals. Usually these systems are fairly complicated, allocating so many points for occupation (an accountant is a much better risk than a cab driver), age, credit out-

POINTS	1
AGE	Under 21
MARITAL STATUS	Separated
DEPENDENTS (including spouse)	7 or more
SALARY (annual)	Under $6,000
WORKING FOR PRESENT EMPLOYER	Under 1 Yr.
HOUSING COSTS	Over $250
HOUSING FACILITIES	Living with parents

standing, bank accounts, etc. But some banks offer forms to enable people to figure for themselves how good or poor a credit risk they are. Such a form is reproduced here. According to the banks, a rating of 15-19 is "very good"; 20-25, "excellent"; 26 or over, "outstanding."

2	3	4	5
21-25	26-36	37-60	Over 60
Divorced	Single	Widowed	Married
5 or 6	3 or 4	1 or 2	None
$6,000-$9,600	$9,600-$12,000	$12,000-$18,000	Over $18,000
1-2 Yrs.	2-5 Yrs.	5-10 Yrs.	Over 10 Yrs.
$201-$250	$125-$200	$75-$124	Under $75
Furnished rental	Unfurnished rental	Own/Mortgage	Own/Free & Clear

THE "RULE OF 78" ON PREPAYMENT OF INSTALLMENT LOANS

On installment loans of all kinds except those on real estate over $25,000 and those for certain agricultural categories, prepayment is governed by the so-called "rule of 78." This cabalistic-sounding formula is one designed to boggle the mind of a non-mathematical-minded borrower. It has to do with the amount of the service charge the bank gets to keep even if you prepay. In brief: the workings of the "rule of 78" indicate that you simply should not prepay because by the time you have made one-third of your payments the bank has already taken more than half of its interest. After payment number four it is advantageous to you to let the installment loan run its course and put into a savings account the money you would have used to prepay your loan.

If you insist on knowing more, attend:

The "78" in the rule stems from the fact that 78 is the number you get when you add up the digits from one through 12; i.e.,

$$1 + 2 + 3 + 4 + 5 + 6 + 7 + 8 + 9 + 10 + 11 + 12$$

Why through 12? Because that is normally the number of payments made on installment loans in a year.

If you prepay after the first month's payment, the bank figures that it has earned 12/78 of the service charge.

If you prepay after the second month, the bank has earned 12/78 + 11/78 or 23/78 of its finance charges.

For loans running to 24 installments, the number used is the sum of 1 through 24, or 300. For 36 installments, the number is 666.

To put all of this into tabular form, figuring on a loan of $1,000 at 6% add-on interest, i.e., finance charges of $60, the loan to be repaid in 12 equal installments, we get something that looks like this:

Loan (amount + finance charges) $1,060.00

Month	Payment $	Finance Charge Earned by Bank in 78's	in %	in $	$ Balance Due	Refundable Finance Charge $
1	88.33	12	15.4	9.24	971.67	50.76
2	88.33	23	29.5	17.70	883.34	42.30
3	88.33	33	42.3	25.38	795.01	34.62
4	88.33	42	53.8	32.28	706.68	27.72
5	88.33	50	64.1	38.46	618.35	21.54
6	88.33	57	73.1	43.86	530.02	16.14
7	88.33	63	80.8	48.48	441.69	11.64
8	88.33	68	87.2	52.32	353.36	7.68
9	88.33	72	92.3	55.38	265.03	4.62
10	88.33	75	96.2	57.72	176.70	2.28
11	88.33	77	98.7	59.22	88.37	.78
12	88.33	78	100.0	60.00	—	—

For a two-year loan
Loan (amount + finance charges) $1,120.00

Month	Payment $	Finance Charge Earned by Bank in 300's	in %	in $	Balance Due $	Refundable Finance Charge $
1	46.67	24	8.0	9.60	1,073.33	110.40
2	46.67	47	15.7	18.84	1,026.66	101.16
3	46.67	69	23.0	27.60	979.99	92.40
4	46.67	90	30.0	36.00	933.32	84.00
5	46.67	110	36.7	44.04	886.65	75.96
6	46.67	129	43.0	51.60	839.98	68.40
7	46.67	147	49.0	58.80	793.31	61.20
8	46.47	164	54.7	65.44	746.64	54.36
9	46.67	180	60.0	72.00	699.97	48.00
10	46.67	195	65.0	78.00	653.30	42.00
11	46.67	209	69.7	83.64	606.63	36.36
12	46.67	222	74.0	88.80	559.96	31.20
13	46.67	234	78.0	93.60	513.29	26.40
14	46.67	245	81.7	98.04	466.62	21.96
15	46.67	255	85.0	102.00	419.95	18.00
16	46.67	264	88.0	105.60	373.28	14.40
17	46.67	272	90.7	108.84	326.61	11.16
18	46.67	279	93.0	111.60	279.94	8.40
19	46.67	285	95.0	114.00	233.27	6.00
20	46.67	290	96.7	116.04	186.60	3.96
21	46.67	294	98.0	117.60	139.93	2.40
22	46.67	297	99.0	118.80	93.26	1.20
23	46.67	299	99.7	119.40	46.59	.60
24	46.59	300	100.0	120.00	—	—

For a three-year loan
Loan (amount + finance charges) $1,180.00

| Month | Payment $ | Finance Charge Earned by Bank | | | Balance Due $ | Refundable Finance Charge $ |
		in 666's	in %	in $		
1	32.78	36	5.4	9.72	1,147.22	170.28
2	32.78	71	10.7	19.26	1,114.44	160.74
3	32.78	105	15.8	28.44	1,081.66	151.56
4	32.78	138	20.7	37.26	1,048.88	142.74
5	32.78	170	25.5	45.90	1,016.10	134.10
6	32.78	201	30.2	54.36	983.32	125.64
7	32.78	231	34.7	62.46	950.54	117.54
8	32.78	260	39.0	70.20	917.76	109.80
9	32.78	288	43.2	77.76	884.98	102.24
10	32.78	315	47.3	85.14	852.20	94.86
11	32.78	341	51.2	92.16	819.42	87.84
12	32.78	366	55.0	99.00	786.64	81.00
13	32.78	390	58.6	105.48	753.86	74.52
14	32.78	413	62.0	111.60	721.08	68.40
15	32.78	435	65.3	117.54	688.30	62.46
16	32.78	456	68.5	123.30	655.52	56.70
17	32.78	476	71.5	128.70	622.74	51.30
18	32.78	495	74.3	133.74	589.96	46.26
19	32.78	513	77.0	138.60	557.18	41.40
20	32.78	530	80.0	144.00	524.40	36.00
21	32.78	546	82.0	147.60	491.62	32.40
22	32.78	561	84.2	151.56	458.84	28.44
23	32.78	575	86.3	155.34	426.06	24.66
24	32.78	588	88.3	158.94	393.28	21.06

continued

For a three-year loan
Loan (amount + finance charges) $1,180.00

| Month | Payment $ | Finance Charge Earned by Bank | | | Balance Due $ | Refundable Finance Charge $ |
		in 666's	in %	in $		
25	32.78	600	90.1	162.18	360.50	17.82
26	32.78	611	91.7	165.06	327.72	14.94
27	32.78	621	93.2	167.76	294.94	12.24
28	32.78	630	94.6	170.28	262.16	9.72
29	32.78	638	95.8	172.44	229.38	7.56
30	32.78	645	96.8	174.24	196.60	5.76
31	32.78	651	97.7	175.86	163.82	4.14
32	32.78	656	98.5	177.30	131.04	2.70
33	32.78	660	99.1	178.38	98.26	1.62
34	32.78	663	99.5	179.10	65.48	.90
35	32.78	665	99.8	179.64	32.70	.36
36	32.70	666	100.0	180.00	—	—

LOAN PROGRESS CHARTS

Showing Dollar Balances Remaining on a Home
Loan for Each $1,000 of the Original Amount at Five-Year Intervals

7% Loan
Original Term in Years

Age of Loan	5	10	15	20	25	30
1 yr.	827	928	961	976	985	990
5 yrs.		586	774	862	911	941
10 yrs.			454	666	786	857
15 yrs.				389	608	738
20 yrs.					356	569
25 yrs.						330

8% Loan
Original Term in Years

Age of Loan	5	10	15	20	25	30
1 yr.	831	932	964	979	987	992
5 yrs.		598	787	875	923	951
10 yrs.			471	688	807	877
15 yrs.				411	635	767
20 yrs.					380	603
25 yrs.						360

9% Loan
Original Term in Years

Age of Loan	5	10	15	20	25	30
1 yr.	834	935	967	981	989	993
5 yrs.		610	800	887	932	959
10 yrs.			487	710	826	894
15 yrs.				432	659	792
20 yrs.					399	633
25 yrs.						384

PERSONAL-LOAN COMPANY
INTEREST RATES BY STATE

Laws governing the operations of personal-loan companies, which charge the highest interest rates except for pawnbrokers, are made by the states. The actual annual interest rates are almost impossible to compare except on an arbitrary basis: the same amount borrowed over the same term and paid back in the same way, in one year with twelve monthly payments. This table makes that comparison on the basis of a $100 loan repaid in 12 monthly installments. It also shows the maximum amount personal finance companies can lend in each state. The range is enormous in this regard: from several hundred dollars to no limit, with numerous variations in between. The actual interest rates vary a great deal also: from a low of just under 15% (Delaware and Georgia) to a chilling high of 62% in Alaska.

MAXIMUM CONSUMER FINANCE RATES

STATE	MAXI-MUM LOAN SIZE	MAXIMUM LOAN RATE (Monthly—except where indicated)		ACTUAL ANNUAL PERCENTAGE RATE $100 Loan—1 Year
Alabama	$300	$1 - $75	$1 per $5	36.00%
		$76 - $200	3%	
		$201 - $300	2%	
Alaska	$1,500	$1 - $50	5%	62.00%
		$51 - $400	3%	
		$401 - $800	2½%	
		$801 - $1,500	1%	
Arizona	$1,000	$1 - $300	3%	45.75%
		$301 - $600	2%	
		$601 - $1,000	1%	
Arkansas	no limit	10% per year simple interest		10.00%
California	no limit	$1 - $200	2½%	30.00%
		$201 - $500	2%	
		$501 - $700	1½%	
		$701 and over	1%	
Colorado	$1,500	$1 - $300	3%	40.25%
		$301 - $500	1½%	
		$501 - $1,500	1%	
Connecticut	$1,800	$1 - $300	$17 per year per $100	25.75%
		$301 - $1,800	$11 per year per $100	
Delaware	$500	6% per year discount +2% fee		14.45%
D. of C.	no limit	1% per month		19.25%
Florida	$600	$1 - $300	3%	45.75%
		$301 - $600	2%	
Georgia	$2,500	8% per year discount + fee not to exceed $8		14.45%
Hawaii	$300	$1 - $100	3½%	50.75%
		$101 - $300	2½%	
Idaho	$1,000	$1 - $300	3%	45.75%
		$301 - $500	2%	
		$501 - $1,000	1%	
Illinois	$800	$1 - $150	3%	45.75%
		$151 - $300	2%	
		$301 - $800	1%	

MAXIMUM CONSUMER FINANCE RATES

STATE	MAXI-MUM LOAN SIZE	MAXIMUM LOAN RATE (Monthly—except where indicated)		ACTUAL ANNUAL PERCENTAGE RATE $100 Loan—1 Year
Indiana	$500	$1 - $150 $151 - $300 $301 - $500	3½% 2½% 1½%	50.75%
Iowa	$1,000	$1 - $150 $151 - $300 $301 - $700 $701 - $1,000	3% 2% 1½% 1%	45.75%
Kansas	$5,000	$1 - $300 $301 - $5,000	3% 10% per year	45.75%
Kentucky	$800	$1 - $150 $151 - $600 $601 - $800	3% 2% 1%	45.75%
Louisiana	$300	$1 - $150 $151 - $300	3½% 2½%	50.75%
Maine	$2,000	$1 - $300 $301 - $2,000	2½% 1½%	40.25%
Maryland	$300	$1 - $300	3%	45.75%
Massachusetts	$1,500	$1 - $200 $201 - $600 $601 - $1,000 $1,001 - $1,500	2½% 2% 1¾% ¾%	40.25%
Michigan	$1,000	$1 - $300 $301 - $1,000	2½% 1¼%	40.25%
Minnesota	$900	$1 - $300 $301 - $600 $601 - $900	2¾% 1½% 1¼%	43.00%
Mississippi	no limit	fee + interest not to exceed 2% per month		22.91%
Missouri	$2,500	$15 per $100 per year not to exceed 2.218% per month		26.62%
Montana	$1,000	$1 - $300 $301 - $500 $501 - $1,000	20% per year 16% per year 12% per year	29.50%
Nebraska	$2,500	$1 - $300 $301 - $500 $501 - $1,000 $1,001 - $2,500	30% per year 24% per year 18% per year 12% per year	40.25%

MAXIMUM CONSUMER FINANCE RATES

STATE	MAXI-MUM LOAN SIZE	MAXIMUM LOAN RATE (Monthly—except where indicated)		ACTUAL ANNUAL PERCENTAGE RATE $100 Loan—1 Year
Nevada	$7,500	$1 - $1,000 $1,001 - $7,500	9% per year 8% per year	36.74%
New Hampshire	$5,000	$1 - $600 $601 - $1,500 $1,501 - $5,000	2% 1½% 1½% entire loan	34.00%
New Jersey	$1,000	$1 - $500 $501 - $1,000	24% per year 22% per year	34.00%
New Mexico	$1,000	$1 - $150 $151 - $300 $301 - $1,000	3% 2½% 1%	45.75%
New York	$1,400	$1 - $100 $101 - $300 $301 - $900 $901 - $1,400	2½% 2% 1½% 1¼%	40.25%
North Carolina	$900	$1 - $300 $301 - $600 $601 - $900	18% per year 10% per year 8% per year	27.00%
North Dakota	$1,000	$1 - $250 $251 - $500 $501 - $750 $751 - $1,000	2½% 2% 1¾% 1½%	40.25%
Ohio	$1,000	$1 - $150 $151 - $300 $301 - $1,000	3% 2% 8% per year	45.75%
Oklahoma	no limit		1½%	27.00%
Oregon	no limit	$1 - $300 $301 - $500 $501 - $1,500 10% per year for more than $1,500	3% 2% 1%	45.75%
Pennsylvania	$600	$1 - $150 $151 - $300 $301 - $600	3% 2% 1%	45.75%
Rhode Island	$2,500	$1 - $300 $301 - $800 $801 - $2,500	3% 2½% 2%	45.75%

MAXIMUM CONSUMER FINANCE RATES

STATE	MAXI-MUM LOAN SIZE	MAXIMUM LOAN RATE (Monthly—except where indicated)		ACTUAL ANNUAL PERCENTAGE RATE $100 Loan—1 Year
South Carolina	$7,500	$1 - $150 on loans over $150: on first $100 $101 - $300 $301 - $1,000 $1,001 - $7,500 + 5% fee or $200 whichever is less	$2.50 per mo. per $100 $20 per year per $100 $18 per year per $100 $9 per year per $100 $7 per year per $100,	44.28%
South Dakota	$2,500	$1 - $300 $301 - $600 $601 - $1,200 $1,201 - $2,500	30% per year 24% per year 18% per year 12% per year	40.00%
Tennessee	no limit	discount + fee less than $20 $5 - $75 on all loans over $75	7½% per year $2 per loan 50¢ per $5 $7.50	30.17%
Texas	$2,500	$1 - $300 $301 - $2,500	$18 per year per $100 $8 per year per $100	27.00%
Utah	$600	$1 - $600	3%	45.75%
Vermont	$1,500	$14 per $100 per year		24.91%
Virginia	$1,000	$1 - $300 $301 - $1,000 — or — $1 - $300 $301 - $1,000	2½% 1½% 17% add-on 12% add-on	40.25%
Washington	$1,000	$1 - $300 $301 - $500 $501 - $1,000	3% 1½% 1%	45.75%
West Virginia	$800	$1 - $100 $101 - $600 $601 - $800	3% 2% 1½%	45.75%
Wisconsin	$300	$1 - $100 $101 - $200 $201 - $300	2½% 2% 1%	40.25%
Wyoming	$1,000	$1 - $150 $151 - $500 $501 - $1,000	3½% 2½% 1%	50.75%

A loan fecklessly and frivolously undertaken becomes an unwanted but very real presence in the house.

HOW MUCH MORTGAGE
A GIVEN AMOUNT OF MONEY CAN BUY

To find the amount of a loan which a specified monthly payment will amortize, multiply the basic monthly payment you can afford by the figure in the appropriate column. The result will be the total loan, expressed in dollars. N.B.: Does not include maintenance, utilities, taxes, etc.

EXAMPLE: A borrower can afford to pay $200 a month for 25 years.

At 7% interest, what amount can he borrow? Read down left-hand column to 25, over to the right to 7% column. Arithmetic: $200 × 141.487 = 28297.40 or a loan of $28,297.40.

TABLE

TIME PERIOD IN YEARS	6½%	7%	7½%	8%	9%
1	11.588	11.571	115.265	114.958	114.350
5	51.109	50.512	49.905	49.318	48.173
10	88.068	86.137	84.245	82.421	78.942
15	114.796	111.256	107.874	104.641	98.593
20	134.126	128.982	124.133	119.554	111.144
25	148.102	141.847	135.320	129.564	119.161
30	158.210	150.308	143.019	136.284	124.282

BUYING A HOME @ 7%
MONTHLY PAYMENT* NECESSARY
TO AMORTIZE THE LOAN

AMOUNT	TERM					
	5 Years	10 Years	15 Years	20 Years	25 Years	30 Years
$ 1,000	19.81	11.62	8.99	7.76	7.07	6.66
$ 5,000	99.01	58.06	44.95	38.77	35.34	33.27
$10,000	198.02	116.11	89.89	77.53	70.68	66.54
$15,000	297.02	174.17	134.83	116.30	106.02	99.80
$20,000	396.03	232.22	179.77	155.06	141.36	133.07
$25,000	495.04	290.28	224.72	193.83	176.70	166.34
$30,000	594.04	348.34	269.66	232.60	212.04	199.60
$40,000	792.06	464.44	359.54	310.12	282.72	266.14

*Does not include a portion of real estate taxes and fire insurance premiums which often are added to monthly payments by mortgagor.

BUYING A HOME AT 8%
MONTHLY PAYMENT* NECESSARY
TO AMORTIZE THE LOAN

AMOUNT			TERM			
	5 Years	10 Years	15 Years	20 Years	25 Years	30 Years
$ 1,000	20.28	12.14	9.56	8.37	7.72	7.34
$ 5,000	101.39	60.67	47.79	41.83	38.60	36.69
$10,000	202.77	121.33	95.57	83.65	77.19	73.38
$15,000	304.15	182.00	143.35	125.47	115.78	110.07
$20,000	405.53	242.66	191.14	167.29	154.37	146.76
$25,000	506.92	303.33	238.93	209.12	192.97	183.45
$30,000	608.30	364.00	286.70	250.94	231.56	220.14
$40,000	811.06	485.32	382.28	334.58	308.74	293.52

*Does not include a portion of real estate taxes and fire insurance premiums which often are added to monthly payments by mortgagor.

BUYING A HOME AT 9%
MONTHLY PAYMENT* NECESSARY
TO AMORTIZE THE LOAN

AMOUNT	TERM					
	5 Years	10 Years	15 Years	20 Years	25 Years	30 Years
$ 1,000	20.76	12.67	10.15	9.00	8.40	8.05
$ 5,000	103.80	63.34	50.72	44.99	41.96	40.24
$10,000	207.59	126.68	101.43	89.98	83.92	80.47
$15,000	311.38	190.02	152.14	134.96	125.88	120.70
$20,000	415.17	253.36	202.86	179.95	167.84	160.93
$25,000	518.97	316.70	253.58	224.94	209.80	201.17
$30,000	622.76	380.04	304.28	269.92	251.76	241.40
$40,000	830.34	506.72	405.72	359.90	335.68	321.86

*Does not include a portion of real estate taxes and fire insurance premiums which often are added to monthly payments by mortgagor.

COMPUTING TRUE INTEREST, OR ANNUAL PERCENTAGE RATE, BY TABLE

On these pages is reproduced one page of a table with instructions on how to use it to determine the Annual Percentage Rate (APR) on an installment purchase. This comes from the Federal Reserve's pamphlet. Full sets of APR tables may be obtained from your nearest Federal Reserve Bank for a modest charge. By using tables of this sort you do not have to apply the true interest formula shown on page 36 of this book.

EXAMPLE

Finance charge = $35.00; Total amount financed = $200; Number of monthly payments = 24.

SOLUTION

Step 1—Divide the finance charge by the total amount financed and multiply by $100. This gives the finance charge per $100 of amount financed. That is, $35.00 ÷ $200 = .1750 × $100 = $17.50.

Step 2—Follow down the left hand column of the table to the line for 24 months. Follow across this line until you find the nearest number to $17.50. In this example $17.51 is closest to $17.50. Reading up the column of figures shows an annual percentage rate of 16%.

ANNUAL PERCENTAGE RATE

NUMBER OF PAY-MENTS	14.00 %	14.25 %	14.50 %	14.75 %	15.00 %	15.25 %	15.50 %	15.75 %
FINANCE CHARGE PER $100 OF AMOUNT FINANCED								
1	1.17	1.19	1.21	1.23	1.25	1.27	1.29	1.31
2	1.75	1.78	1.82	1.85	1.88	1.91	1.94	1.97
3	2.34	2.38	2.43	2.47	2.51	2.55	2.59	2.64
4	2.93	2.99	3.04	3.09	3.14	3.20	3.25	3.30
5	3.53	3.59	3.65	3.72	3.78	3.84	3.91	3.97
6	4.12	4.20	4.27	4.35	4.42	4.49	4.57	4.64
7	4.72	4.81	4.89	4.98	5.06	5.15	5.23	5.32
8	5.32	5.42	5.51	5.61	5.71	5.80	5.90	6.00
9	5.92	6.03	6.14	6.25	6.35	6.46	6.57	6.68
10	6.53	6.65	6.77	6.88	7.00	7.12	7.24	7.36
11	7.14	7.27	7.40	7.53	7.66	7.79	7.92	8.05
12	7.74	7.89	8.03	8.17	8.31	8.45	8.59	8.74
13	8.36	8.51	8.66	8.81	8.97	9.12	9.27	9.43
14	8.97	9.13	9.30	9.46	9.63	9.79	9.96	10.12
15	9.59	9.76	9.94	10.11	10.29	10.47	10.64	10.82
16	10.20	10.39	10.58	10.77	10.95	11.14	11.33	11.52
17	10.82	11.02	11.22	11.42	11.62	11.82	12.02	12.22
18	11.45	11.66	11.87	12.08	12.29	12.50	12.72	12.93
19	12.07	12.30	12.52	12.74	12.97	13.19	13.41	13.64
20	12.70	12.93	13.17	13.41	13.64	13.88	14.11	14.35
21	13.33	13.58	13.82	14.07	14.32	14.57	14.82	15.06
22	13.96	14.22	14.48	14.74	15.00	15.26	15.52	15.78
23	14.59	14.87	15.14	15.68	15.96	16.23	16.50	16.78
24	15.23	15.51	15.80	16.08	16.37	16.65	16.94	17.22
25	15.87	16.17	16.46	16.76	17.06	17.35	17.65	17.95
26	16.51	16.82	17.13	17.44	17.75	18.06	18.37	18.68
27	17.15	17.47	17.80	18.12	18.44	18.76	19.09	19.41
28	17.80	18.13	18.47	18.80	19.14	19.47	19.81	20.15
29	18.45	18.79	19.14	19.49	19.83	20.18	20.53	20.88
30	19.10	19.45	19.81	20.17	20.54	20.90	21.26	21.62

ANNUAL PERCENTAGE RATE

FINANCE CHARGE PER $100 OF AMOUNT FINANCED

16.00 %	16.25 %	16.50 %	16.75 %	17.00 %	17.25 %	17.50 %	17.75 %	NUMBER OF PAY-MENTS
1.23	1.35	1.37	1.40	1.42	1.44	1.46	1.48	1
2.00	2.04	2.07	2.10	2.13	2.16	2.19	2.22	2
2.68	2.72	2.76	2.80	2.85	2.89	2.93	2.97	3
3.36	3.41	3.46	3.51	3.57	3.62	3.67	3.73	4
4.04	4.10	4.16	4.23	4.29	4.35	4.42	4.48	5
4.72	4.79	4.87	4.94	5.02	5.09	5.17	5.24	6
5.40	5.49	5.58	5.66	5.75	5.83	5.92	6.00	7
6.09	6.19	6.29	6.38	6.48	6.58	6.67	6.77	8
6.78	6.89	7.00	7.11	7.22	7.32	7.43	7.54	9
7.48	7.60	7.72	7.84	7.96	8.08	8.19	8.31	10
8.18	8.31	8.44	8.57	8.70	8.83	8.96	9.09	11
8.88	9.02	9.16	9.30	9.45	9.59	9.73	9.87	12
9.58	9.73	9.89	10.04	10.20	10.35	10.50	10.66	13
10.29	10.45	10.62	10.78	10.95	11.11	11.28	11.45	14
11.00	11.17	11.35	11.53	11.71	11.88	12.06	12.24	15
11.71	11.90	12.09	12.28	12.46	12.65	12.84	13.03	16
12.42	12.62	12.83	13.03	13.23	13.43	13.63	13.83	17
13.14	13.35	13.57	13.78	13.99	14.21	14.42	14.64	18
13.86	14.09	14.31	14.54	14.76	14.99	15.22	15.44	19
14.59	14.82	15.06	15.30	15.54	15.77	16.01	16.25	20
15.31	15.56	15.81	16.06	16.31	16.56	16.81	17.07	21
16.04	16.30	16.57	16.83	17.09	17.36	17.62	17.88	22
16.78	17.05	17.32	17.60	17.88	18.15	18.43	18.70	23
17.51	17.80	18.09	18.37	18.66	18.95	19.24	19.53	24
18.25	18.55	18.85	19.15	19.45	19.75	20.05	20.36	25
18.99	19.30	19.62	19.93	20.24	20.56	20.87	21.19	26
19.74	20.06	20.39	20.71	21.04	21.37	21.69	22.02	27
20.48	20.82	21.16	21.50	21.84	22.18	22.52	22.86	28
21.23	21.58	21.94	22.29	22.64	22.99	23.35	23.70	29
21.99	22.35	22.72	23.08	23.45	23.81	24.18	24.55	30

ANNUAL PERCENTAGE RATE

NUMBER OF PAY- MENTS	14.00 %	14.25 %	14.50 %	14.75 %	15.00 %	15.25 %	15.50 %	15.75 %
FINANCE CHARGE PER $100 OF AMOUNT FINANCED								
31	19.75	20.12	20.49	20.87	21.24	21.61	21.99	22.37
32	20.40	20.79	21.17	21.56	21.95	22.33	22.72	23.11
33	21.06	21.46	21.85	22.25	22.65	23.06	23.46	23.86
34	21.72	22.13	22.54	22.95	23.37	23.78	24.19	24.61
35	22.38	22.80	23.23	23.65	24.08	24.51	24.94	25.36
36	23.04	23.48	23.92	24.35	24.80	25.24	25.68	26.12
37	23.70	24.16	24.61	25.06	25.51	25.97	26.42	26.88
38	24.37	24.84	25.30	25.77	26.24	26.70	27.17	27.64
39	25.04	25.52	26.00	26.48	26.96	27.44	27.92	28.41
40	25.71	26.20	26.70	27.19	27.69	28.18	28.68	29.18
41	26.39	26.89	27.40	27.91	28.41	28.92	29.44	29.95
42	27.06	27.58	28.10	28.62	29.15	29.67	30.19	30.72
43	27.74	28.27	28.81	29.34	29.88	30.42	30.96	31.50
44	28.42	28.97	29.52	30.07	30.62	31.17	31.72	32.28
45	29.11	29.67	30.23	30.79	31.36	31.92	32.49	33.06
46	29.79	30.36	30.94	31.52	32.10	32.68	33.26	33.84
47	30.48	31.07	31.66	32.25	32.84	33.44	34.03	34.63
48	31.17	31.77	32.37	32.98	33.59	34.20	34.81	35.42
49	31.86	32.48	33.09	33.71	34.34	34.96	35.59	36.21
50	32.55	33.18	33.82	34.45	35.09	35.73	36.37	37.01
51	33.25	33.89	34.54	35.19	35.84	36.49	37.15	37.81
52	33.95	34.61	35.27	35.93	36.60	37.27	37.94	38.61
53	34.65	35.32	36.00	36.68	37.36	38.04	38.72	39.41
54	35.35	36.04	36.73	37.42	38.12	38.82	39.52	40.22
55	36.05	36.76	37.46	38.17	38.88	39.60	40.31	41.03
56	36.76	37.48	38.20	38.92	39.65	40.38	41.11	41.84
57	37.47	38.20	38.94	39.68	40.42	41.16	41.91	42.65
58	38.18	38.93	39.68	40.43	41.19	41.95	42.71	43.47
59	38.89	39.66	40.42	41.19	41.96	42.74	43.51	44.29
60	39.61	40.39	41.17	41.95	42.74	43.53	44.32	45.11

ANNUAL PERCENTAGE RATE

16.00 %	16.25 %	16.50 %	16.75 %	17.00 %	17.25 %	17.50 %	17.75 %	NUMBER OF PAY-MENTS
FINANCE CHARGE PER $100 OF AMOUNT FINANCED								
22.74	23.12	23.50	23.88	24.26	24.64	25.02	25.40	31
23.50	23.89	24.28	24.68	25.07	25.46	25.86	26.25	32
24.26	24.67	25.07	25.48	25.88	26.29	26.70	27.11	33
25.03	25.44	25.86	26.28	26.70	27.12	27.54	27.97	34
25.79	26.23	26.66	27.09	27.52	27.96	28.39	28.83	35
26.57	27.01	27.46	27.90	28.35	28.80	29.25	29.70	36
27.34	27.80	28.26	28.72	29.18	29.64	30.10	30.57	37
28.11	28.59	29.06	29.53	30.01	30.49	30.96	31.44	38
28.89	29.38	29.87	30.36	30.85	31.34	31.83	32.32	39
29.68	30.18	30.68	31.18	31.68	32.19	32.69	33.20	40
30.46	30.97	31.49	32.01	32.52	33.04	33.56	34.08	41
31.25	31.78	32.31	32.84	33.37	33.90	34.44	34.97	42
32.04	32.58	33.13	33.67	34.22	34.76	35.31	35.86	43
32.83	33.39	33.95	34.51	35.07	35.63	36.19	36.76	44
33.63	34.20	34.77	35.35	35.92	36.50	37.08	37.66	45
34.43	35.01	35.60	36.19	36.78	37.37	37.96	38.56	46
35.23	35.83	36.43	37.04	37.64	38.25	38.86	39.46	47
36.03	36.65	37.27	37.88	38.50	39.13	39.75	40.37	48
36.84	37.47	38.10	38.74	39.37	40.01	40.65	41.29	49
37.65	38.30	38.94	39.59	40.24	40.89	41.55	42.20	50
38.46	39.12	39.79	40.45	41.11	41.78	42.45	43.12	51
39.28	39.96	40.63	41.31	41.99	42.67	43.36	44.04	52
40.10	40.79	41.48	42.17	42.87	43.57	44.27	44.97	53
40.92	41.63	42.33	43.04	43.75	44.47	45.18	45.90	54
41.74	42.47	43.19	43.91	44.64	45.37	46.10	46.83	55
42.57	43.31	44.05	44.79	45.53	46.27	47.02	47.77	56
43.40	44.15	44.91	45.66	46.42	47.18	47.94	48.71	57
44.23	45.00	45.77	46.54	47.32	48.09	48.87	49.65	58
45.07	45.85	46.64	47.42	48.21	49.01	49.80	50.60	59
45.91	46.71	47.51	48.31	49.12	49.92	50.73	51.55	60

GLOSSARY

A

add-on interest rate

This is interest computed *on* and then *added to* the original amount as the new principal. It is commonly used in installment loans.

amortized mortgage loan

A loan in which the debt—principal and interest—is reduced by a series of fixed payments at equal intervals. The periodic payment is greater than the interest for any period, so part of the payment is from the beginning applied to reduction of the principal. As the principal is gradually reduced, the interest per period decreases, so a larger portion of the periodic payment begins to be applied to amortization.

amount   The total of a principal plus interest.

annual percentage rate   The actual effective interest based on annual percentage (APR) tables, or the interest stated in terms of simple interest.

B

balloon payment   A final, and higher payment than the earlier periodic ones, made on a real estate loan. Frequently used in agreements covering second mortgages, also in commercial mortgages.

banks   Financial institutions which accept and hold deposits, make loans and investments. Essentially each function is an exchange of credit for money or of money for credit.

bankruptcy   The state or condition of one who is unable to pay his debts. The property of a bankrupt may be seized by creditors, acting through a trustee under federal court order.

blue-chip stocks	Financial jargon referring to the common stocks of America's most respected companies—those which have the highest ratings. Examples: General Motors, Standard Oil of New Jersey, General Foods.
bonds	Certificates that are evidence of debt owed by a corporation or a government, issued for the purpose of borrowing money. The issuer promises to return to the bondholder the principal sum borrowed when the bond matures at some future date. Bonds state a fixed rate of interest which is usually paid to the bondholder semi-annually.
business loan	Credit granted to a business firm, usually to finance purchases of inventory and/or equipment, or to enable the company to meet other short-term money requirements.

C

capital investment	Funds spent by businesses for new or modernized plants,

equipment, fixtures and other items known as fixed assets. Usually the purpose is to expand production capacity in order to increase sales volume.

carrying charges

The cost of servicing a loan. Includes the charges a lender makes to cover his risk, pay his administrative costs, keep payment records, and compute interest.

chattel mortgage

A lien or claim which secures small loans granted by a consumer finance company. The chattel mortgage — the word comes originally from "cattle" —is an attachment on movable personal property (i.e., excluding land) such as automobiles, appliances, furniture, etc.

This property can be seized by the creditor if the debtor defaults.

check

A written promise or order to pay a definite sum of money to a named payee. It is a credit instrument drawn on a bank, based upon the drawer's deposit with the bank.

closing costs

Fees payable upon the exchange of title to real estate, other than the cost of the property. Examples: fees for recording property title; fees for holding money in escrow; change of ownership fees; pro-rated taxes; insurance.

collateral

Any tangible asset, usually marketable securities or life insurance, pledged as security for a loan.

commercial banks

Financial institutions which hold demand deposits and honor checks drawn upon them, and lend money to individuals and companies for various purposes. Commercial banks buy and hold government and municipal bonds, and also offer services in competition with other savings institutions.

compound interest

Interest paid on a principal which grows periodically as

a result of prior interest being added to and becoming part of the principal.

consolidating loans   The practice of lumping together various debts so that the borrower makes one monthly or weekly payment rather than many separate ones.

consumer credit   Credit extended to the ultimate purchaser, i.e., for personal rather than commercial use.

credit   The ability to acquire goods or services now on a promise to pay in the future.

credit markets   Various sources of loans available to consumers.

D

deadbeat   Trade slang for a questionable credit risk. One who is likely to avoid meeting his obligations when due.

declining balance   A type of mortgage calling for a fixed amount being paid on the principal at regular intervals. Usually interest is assessed on this ever-declining balance rather than on the original principal.

default   To fail to meet an obligation, e.g., a mortgage payment.

depression   A breakdown in a nation's economy, including a collapse of production, lower business and personal income, lower prices, reduced lending activity, high unemployment, many business failures.

disability insurance   A policy that provides tax-exempt income when an insured person is disabled either by an accident or by illness.

discount interest   Interest paid in advance. For example, 5% discount interest results in a $100 loan owed, but only $95 advanced to the borrower.

E

escrow   When money is deposited with a third party as part of a contract between two other parties and held until the conditions are met — e.g., mortgage papers are drawn up and signed—the money is in escrow.

F

finance company   A state-regulated consumer loan company. Doing business under state law, finance companies must be licensed and bonded, and are subject to supervision.

foreclose   Seizure of property by court order when the mortgage is not repaid on time or if any conditions of the loan contract are not satisfied. Usually the property then is sold to satisfy the mortgage debt.

franchise   A privilege granted for a fee to an individual by a manufacturer or service corporation to permit a product to be sold in a given area. For ex-

ample, an automobile manufacturer grants a dealer a franchise to sell his make of car.

G

garnishment A legal process by which a portion of the wages or salary of a debtor may be withheld by an employer for payment of debts.

garnishee To effect garnishment (*above*).

gross income Total income; earnings before payroll deductions.

guarantor One who pledges to pay for a debt incurred by another if necessary.

H

holder in due course A person who is legally entitled to payment of a bill, note or check.

I

interest A monetary consideration for the use of invested or loaned capital, expressed as a percent of the principal over a definite period of time, usually one year.

inflation   A decline in value of a currency, accompanied by a rise in prices of goods and services, caused in part by an increase in the amount of currency in circulation. Inflation also may be caused when the supply of goods fails to meet the demand.

installment plan   Credit extended, usually for the purchase of higher-priced consumers' goods, and paid off in periodic installments until it is liquidated at the maturity of the contract. The legal document used in connection with an installment sale is usually either a chattel mortgage or a conditional bill of sale. Title to the goods is retained by the seller until the final payment has been made; or by a financial institution to which he has sold the mortgage or bill of sale.

itemized deductions   The costs of doing business and amounts spent by individual taxpayers which the U.S. Internal Revenue Service permits to be made as deductions against ordinary income, before taxes are calculated. For a company, a tax-deductible item would be, say, interest paid to its bondholders; for an individual, examples would be hospital expenses, real estate taxes, automobile expenses when a car is used for business purposes.

L

loan assignment   The transfer of a claim, right, or property of a borrower to certain persons called assignees. The assignees then have control over whatever has been transferred.

loan shark   An unlicensed lender who charges usurious interest rates, often from 300% upward. These lenders may even refuse to accept payments on the principal until the full amount owed can be made in one payment, thus keeping their illegal loans outstanding continuously and extracting maximum interest.

M

mutual savings banks   State-chartered institutions whose depositors own shares of the bank and receive "dividends" rather than interest. The banks accept only time deposits, invest primarily in real estate loans.

O

open-end mortgage   A pledge of real property to a creditor which permits periodic lump sum payments to be made on the principal without penalty to the mortgagee.

P

personal loan   Usually a loan secured by a chattel mortgage on consumer goods or the signature of one or two "co-signers" who may be friends of the borrower.

prepayment Paying a portion of or all of an outstanding loan in advance of its due date.

principal Amount of capital originally invested or borrowed.

R

recession A period of economic contraction similar to but less severe than a depression.

S

savings and loan association An institution which devotes its assets to urban mortgage banking almost exclusively. These banks are also popular places for personal savings deposits because they pay higher interest rates than commercial banks.

second mortgage A lien, usually against real estate, which is subordinate to a first mortgage on the property. Because they are not the primary loans which finance the purchases, second mortgages usually carry higher interest rates and may require balloon payments. If the mortgagee defaults, the holder of a second mortgage gets nothing until the claims of the first mortgage are fully satisfied.

security   An asset given as a pledge of repayment or fulfillment of a debt. One example would be shares of stock deposited as collateral for a bank loan.

securities   A generic term referring to common stocks, preferred stocks, bonds, mutual funds, etc.

service charge   A fee separate and apart from normal interest charges.

service contract   A written agreement which states the terms of service to be applied for a durable goods purchase.

simple interest   Interest computed only on the original principal, which

remains unchanged throughout the term of the loan.

straight life insurance   A policy with an unchanging premium payable during the lifetime of the insured. Also called ordinary life or whole life, this policy has a cash value.

stocks   Common stocks technically represent the equity in, or residual ownership of, a corporation, and possess the element of control through voting power. Their value may go up or down as they are traded, and they may or may not pay dividends.

T

term   The length of a loan, usually expressed in months or years.

term insurance   A policy which pays death benefits but has no cash value.

tight money   When credit is scarce and/or expensive. Mortgages, consumer loans and bank collateral loans become difficult to obtain when money is tight.

time contract   A loan agreement such as an installment contract, in which periodic payments clear the debt by a specified maturity date.

truth-in-lending law   Requires banks and other lenders to state the actual effective annual interest rate (APR) on all loans. Also known as Regulation Z.

U

unsecured loan   Credit extended to a borrower only on the strength of his signature and financial statement.

W

working capital   The excess of a company's current assets over its current liabilities. For an individual, working capital constitutes the cash he has available, and his ability to turn assets owned into cash in a relatively short time.

INDEX

ACKNOWLEDGMENTS

The editors of Dreyfus Publications wish to thank Robert P. Shay, Professor of Banking and Finance, Graduate School of Business, Columbia University, for his helpful commentary on the manuscript; Joe Argenziano, of Argenziano Associates, and Dan Sibley, graphics consultant, for assistance in preparing promotion materials; David M. Glixon and Max M. Stein of The George Macy Companies, for editorial production; Thomas W. Diehl, Instructor, University of California at San Diego Extension, for materials used in Chapter XIII and the Glossary; and Spero Yianilos for pinch-hitting in too many departments to list.